Living with the

RESCUES

Living with the
RESCUES

LIFE LESSONS AND INSPIRATIONS

Sharon Langford

GREENLEAF
BOOK GROUP PRESS

Published by Greenleaf Book Group Press
Austin, Texas
www.gbgpress.com

Distributed by Greenleaf Book Group LLC

For ordering information or special discounts for bulk purchases, please contact Greenleaf Book Group LLC at PO Box 91869, Austin, TX 78709, 512.891.6100.

Design and composition by Greenleaf Book Group LLC
Cover design by Greenleaf Book Group LLC

Photos by Remember This Photography:
Pages 1, 2, 3, 4, 5, 6, 16, 25, 31, 34, 35, 36, 38, 41, 43, 47, 48, 50, 67, 68, 73, 75

Photos by Grannis Photography:
Pages 15, 23, 27, 28, 44, 98

Publisher's Cataloging-In-Publication Data
(Prepared by The Donohue Group, Inc.)

Langford, Sharon.
  Living with the rescues : life lessons and inspirations / Sharon Langford. -- 1st ed.

  p. : ill. ; cm.

  ISBN: 978-1-60832-045-5

1. Dog rescue. 2. Dog adoption. 3. Dogs--Anecdotes. 4. Human-animal relationships--Anecdotes. I. Title.

HV4746 .L36 2010
636.832   2010922925

Part of the Tree Neutral™ program, which offsets the number of trees consumed in the production and printing of this book by taking proactive steps, such as planting trees in direct proportion to the number of trees used: www.treeneutral.com

Printed in the China on acid-free paper

10 11 12 13 14 15 10 9 8 7 6 5 4 3 2 1

First Edition

Dedicated to the memory of **DAISY**, my first rescue dog.

All proceeds from the sale of this book go to Daisy's Legacy, a trust established to help special needs animals.

Thank you for buying this book and helping animals. Here are some other ways you can help:
- Adopt an animal from a shelter.
- Volunteer with an organization to help animals.
- Contribute financially to organizations that help animals.
- Spay and neuter your pets.
- Support animal welfare legislation.
- Buy more copies of this book, give them to friends and family, and recommend the book to others.

I WROTE THIS BOOK hoping that it would inspire readers to find a place in their hearts and homes for one or more homeless animals.

I came to realize in the last few months that I had reached my limit in the amount of time and money I had available to help animals. In addition to caring for eight dogs, I was also providing some "scholarships" for dogs my friends and I have placed in good homes. I have also made financial commitments to some organizations that help animals.

I felt very challenged because so many animals need homes. Then the idea to write about the dogs came to me—and persisted. I decided to write this book and donate all the proceeds to benefit animals.

A lot of people get involved when there is an emergency situation like a natural disaster or a puppy mill rescue. (Sometimes breeders confine dogs to crowded, often unsanitary, environments with inadequate care and no socialization. Authorities close such facilities and place animals in shelters and foster homes.) Usually these people are not involved on a daily basis. I hope this book will make people realize how much they are needed and how much joy and satisfaction they can receive from adopting a homeless animal. It has been my experience that we see the best and the worst of humanity in how we treat animals. I believe many people would be willing to help once they realize just how much they are needed.

I HAVE A PASSION for and a commitment to special needs dogs. I define *special needs* as emotional and health issues. For example, two of my dogs, Ladye and The Tramp, are so emotionally bonded that they need to stay together. I am passionate about caring for special needs dogs because it gives these dogs a chance to have a good life. My commitment is evolving as I experience the joy of living with Hannah, Barney, Sandy, Rusty, Zeeke, Rocky, Ladye, and The Tramp.

Zeeke and me in dog room

Most dogs in shelters waiting for homes are not special needs dogs and just want love and companionship.

Quite a number of people have told me that they want to come back in their next life as one of my dogs. A few people have suggested—with some humor—that I need "professional" help because of my lifestyle, but living with the dogs seems normal and right to me. I would choose being home in the evenings to serve their dinner and spend time with them over going out for other activities.

Likewise, I think the money I spend for their care is an excellent investment, and it brings me more enjoyment than buying things ever could. Most of us make our decisions based on return on investment, and I receive a huge return on the time and money I spend with the dogs.

I frequently hear dog lovers refer to themselves as "mommy" and "daddy" when talking to their dogs, but I choose to think of the

Donnie Lambert, who did the stonework on my house and grounds and knew about my love for the dogs, surprised me with this.

dogs I live with as friends and companions rather than canine children. I find their companionship very enjoyable and their behavior toward each other and me incredibly interesting.

In the beginning of each of our relationships, I felt a lot of compassion (even pity) for these homeless animals, many of whom had suffered physical and/or emotional abuse. But each dog has been transformed by living an abundant life. They entertain me and inspire me to remember what is really important.

Eight rescue dogs share my home with me—yes, eight! Sometimes there is even a ninth rescue here temporarily, in the process of being transitioned to a new home. We live in a house that I had built on the farm where I lived as a child. My brother Samuel, his wife Cindy, their daughters

Jordan and Raeanna, their five dogs (four of which are rescue), and two rescue cats also live on the farm.

Taking care of eight dogs is a challenge but mostly a joy. I sometimes joke with friends about owning and running a small kennel.

My "management" style with the dogs is the same style I employ with the people in the company where I work, one that few, if any, dog trainers would endorse. I see my role as taking care of them and giving them the freedom to be who they are, and my goal is to have a harmonious, peaceful environment with tolerance, acceptance, respect, and love. I only intervene with the dogs if behavior is negative or potentially dangerous, and I reward/reinforce good behavior with praise, petting, and treats.

My house and grounds were designed to accommodate the special needs and pleasures of the dogs. We have about three acres with cross fencing and gates to provide flexibility for creating separate areas.

The front faces cattle pastures, and woods run along the back fence, so the dogs have lots of other animals to see, hear, and smell—and for their barking pleasure.

This is a James Thurber quote and one of our favorite "canine sayings" in Hannah's and Rocky's special room.

A special room was built in a finished area of the basement as a "safe" place for Hannah and Rocky. It is where they stay when I am not at home and where they sleep. Crates, beds, and toys are available for their enjoyment.

I don't know if aesthetics are important to dogs but we painted the walls of the special room and tiled the floor, and Patti Ross, a local artist, added a rendering of each of the dogs and some of our favorite canine wisdom.

The dog room

The room was constructed of concrete blocks and a steel door to protect Hannah from injury because when/if she gets scared, she tries to get out by scratching, clawing, and trying to climb. To keep things calm, the room is almost soundproof, a ventilation fan makes a continuous noise, and a radio is tuned to a station that plays classical music most of the time. The construction materials, fan, and radio muffle loud noises and thunder. This room is directly under my bedroom so I can hear if Hannah gets upset during the night.

Doggie Condos in garage for Ladye and The Tramp and Barney

We also built a dog room on the main level, which has kennel areas for feeding and a customized shower to make bathing dogs easier. The room includes cabinets for storing food, treats, medicine, and towels. The walls in this room are also practically covered with canine art.

We also built "condos" in the garage and connected a row of doghouses in one of the fenced areas and added a covered porch. A large unfinished area in the basement, which was originally intended for storage, serves as temporary quarters for dogs in transition to new homes. Ladye, The Tramp, and Barney stayed there during the hot summer afternoons until we added air-conditioning in the garage for their condos. The house was an item of curiosity and speculation among some contractors and other spectators. The canine-dedicated space seemed disproportionate to other features of our home—like the small kitchen and the absence of a dining room. The amount of fencing seemed excessive to some.

Fenced area facing pasture

I have a very demanding job as the CEO of a large real estate company and commute into our offices several days a week. To manage the job and the dogs, I have to be well organized, with systems for maintaining food, treats, and medicine inventories. I also have to have schedules, routines, and help when I am away for the day. I order all-natural dog foods, supplements, and treats from Dizzy's Dog Wash and Corner Store in Nashville, Tennessee. Lynn, the owner, is very knowledgeable and has helped me choose just the right foods, supplements, and treats. In particular, I buy Pinnacle dog food, Buddy Biscuits, Liquid Health K9 Glucosamine, and DGP—a holistic supplement for arthritis. When I pick the dogs up from being groomed at Copyright Pet Resort, I schedule the next appointment so I have it on my calendar a month in advance.

Several years ago my small inner voice, which we all have, began whispering—and later shouting—to me that I needed to live closer to nature. I made the decision that I would move from my Green Hills neighborhood in Nashville to our family farm. My spirit needed to be in a more natural environment, and I wanted to

Hannah and me in the dog room

live closer to my family. It was a good and practical decision for the dogs and me—especially after Hannah joined us—and the move made it possible for me to give Barney a home. I work from my home office some days so I can spend more time with all of them.

Our mornings begin early: Before I get ready for work there are four separate feedings and two bathroom outings. I don't set an alarm clock, and the dogs don't wear watches, but they always know when it is time to get up.

If I don't move fast enough, Barney will bark and remind me that it is time for their breakfast. There is no sleeping in, but I sometimes go back to bed on the weekends after everybody has had breakfast and Zeeke and Rocky have gone to the bathroom. Hannah usually will not go out early in the morning.

Ladye, The Tramp, and Barney eat first. I stay with them until breakfast is finished because Ladye and Barney eat quickly and The Tramp eats more slowly; Ladye would "share" The Tramp's food if I were not there. This also gives me special time with each of them. I mix some baby food (rotating sweet potato, macaroni and cheese, and oatmeal) in The Tramp's food. After Barney and Ladye finish eating, they take turns eating tiny bits of baby food from a spoon while The Tramp finishes his meal. I often think about how Ladye was hit by an automobile and left to die on a rural road and how

Barney was living when he came into my life. It gives me such joy to see them as they are now!

Sandy and Rusty eat next. They live in the separated area with connected doghouses and a covered porch. Both are very serious about food, so I have to wait until they finish eating before I can give each one some special attention. They are best buddies except at breakfast and dinner.

Next come Zeeke, Hannah, and Rocky. I prepare their food and serve Zeeke in his kennel in the dog room, and then I take the food for Hannah and Rocky to their room downstairs. After Hannah and Rocky finish eating, I take Rocky (and Hannah if she will go) out for a bathroom break and then get them settled back in their room. I then take Zeeke out for his bathroom break. This routine is repeated in the evening except that Hannah and Rocky eat with Zeeke if the weather is good.

For several weeks after we moved, six of the dogs slept in the bedroom with me. The door had to be closed to keep everyone inside the room because The Tramp and Barney disassemble anything that is stuffed, and Ladye had never totally mastered the inside bathroom. The Tramp slept in the bed with me and sometimes Ladye did too. Hannah had to be in her crate. Zeeke, Rocky, and Barney slept on dog beds, which almost covered the entire surface of the bedroom floor. The idea of having this many dogs sleeping with me is very emotionally appealing but extremely impractical; my bedroom quickly became uninhabitable from the dirt and smells the dogs brought with them.

With encouragement from my sister, Ruth, and Darryl and Blanchard, who were finishing the house, I decided to transition Ladye, The Tramp, and Barney from sleeping in the house with me to sleeping in their condos in the garage or their doghouse.

It was very hard for me to move Ladye and The Tramp out of the house because they had always slept inside. My rational mind told me that they had their choice of condos in the garage or their large house, which has a window and covered porch and is located at the far end of the patio, adjacent to their side yard and near my bedroom. Plus, they like being outside.

I am sure this arrangement bothers me much more than it does them. For instance, they sometimes stare in at me longingly through the glass exterior door that opens on to the patio for long periods of time, but then suddenly they run off barking at something. Most of the time at night they are not nearby when I tiptoe to the backdoor and peek out. But when they are, I feel terrible and usually go outside and pet them; they have the most irresistible faces. I always promise them that they can live in the house when they are seniors if they want to. In the meantime, they seem to have completely adjusted to their living arrangement.

This sign hangs at the entrance to our patio area. (Author unknown.)

Until recently Hannah, Zeeke, and Rocky slept in the bedroom with me, but Hannah had to be crated because of her anxiety. When we had storms or other loud noises, I had to crawl into her crate, pull her out, carry her down to her safe room, medicate her, and hold her until the medicine helped her calm down. This was very difficult and not good for either of us. It was also a battle in the mornings to get her downstairs when I was leaving the house.

I decided it would be better to be consistent. Hannah and Rocky are excited in the evenings now when I say, "Ready to go to your special place?"

Not long ago, Hannah and Rocky confirmed their preference for sleeping in their "special" room. Hannah was in her crate in my bedroom, and Rocky was on his bed in my closet. I had planned to let them sleep with Zeeke and me. I was going to be home the following day, and there were no storms in the forecast. I had been reading, and then I went outside to give Ladye, The Tramp, and Barney their goodnight treats. When I was getting ready to go to bed, both Hannah and Rocky got up and walked toward the stairs leading to their room. I said, "Want to go to your special place?" and they started downstairs with no further prompting.

They have the freedom to sleep in crates or on the bed of their choice and drink water when they want. I miss having them in the room with me at night, particularly their sighs and snoring, but this arrangement is best for them. Hannah still has a crate in my bedroom, which she uses when we all take a nap and when I am at home during the day. Zeeke continues to sleep in the bedroom with me and loves the attention and his unique status.

Every day is a "big hair" day for us. Our home has an abundance of hair on the floors and most surfaces. Zeeke, Rocky, and Hannah get brushed regularly and a de-shed bath every four weeks. Ladye and The Tramp get de-shed baths every six weeks, but you can always find hair in the garage and on the patio. I have a vacuum that is specially designed for dog hair. But no matter how frequently I use it, you can almost always see dog hair blowing across the floor. Unmanageable amounts of hair, nose prints on the glass doors and windows, and torn screens are all minor inconveniences when compared to the amount of joy I get from living with my canine friends.

I am very blessed with people who help me take care of the dogs. My closest office is more than an hour away and the farthest is more than a two-hour drive, so a very special lady, Geovanna, who works on the farm taking care of the baby calves, comes during the days when I am away to take the indoor dogs out to the bathroom and to give treats and attention to all the dogs. If the weather is stormy, she also comes to give Hannah and Rocky their sedatives. She handled taking Sandy to be spayed and Rusty to be neutered and taking the dogs for medical exams and vaccinations before our veterinarian, Dr. Denton Colwell, opened his practice and began making house calls. My sister Ruth is backup to Geovanna. Dr. Colwell now comes to our home specifically to treat Barney, Rusty, and Sandy. He is also adamant that we may call on him at any time.

All of the eight dogs except one have lived on the street. I have them because they needed a home and there was no one else to take them. They all respect the specific order in which they are petted and given treats and food:

1. In the morning, Ladye requires all of my attention first (followed by The Tramp and Barney), but Barney gets food first (followed by Ladye and The Tramp together). Ladye and The Tramp get their treats before Barney does. They accept this sequence and honor it.
2. When Hannah and Rocky eat with Zeeke, Hannah is served first, followed by Rocky and Zeeke; they never try to change the order. These three have a specific kennel and always go there.
3. Zeeke gets brushed first, then Hannah, then Rocky, and they always present themselves in that order.
4. When I drive into the garage, Ladye and The Tramp are petted first, followed by Barney, and they get "coming home"

treats in that sequence.

5. Sandy gets her food first ahead of Rusty. As excited as Rusty is about food, he nevertheless accepts this routine, which means Sandy also gets her treats before he does.

All of the dogs except Zeeke and Rocky (who was named by Collie Rescue) came to me without names. I don't know their ages or their pasts. I am sure that Zeeke and Rocky are seniors, and we give Zeeke the privileges of "seniority." I think Hannah, Ladye, The Tramp, and Barney are middle aged. Sandy and Rusty, based on appearance and behavior, are quite young.

Their interactions with one another are always interesting, as you'll come to see when you read each dog's chapter. For example, Hannah, Rocky, The Tramp, and Barney love to run the fence with Sandy and Rusty. Hannah and The Tramp are incredibly fast runners and chase each other. Ladye adores Zeeke and has since the moment they met. Rocky is not very social with the other dogs except to join in the barking. Barney does not play even though Hannah and Ladye have tried to engage him with play bows and running. Zeeke and Hannah wrestle and play in the house.

I rarely travel or go out in the evenings because of the commitment to take care of the dogs but that's okay with me. They are inspiring and entertaining company.

I love all animals—so much so that I have been a vegetarian for many years. It seems that taking care of dogs is the best way I can help animals, and the dogs just keep showing up in my life. I understand how people—motivated by love and because so many animals need homes—can become animal hoarders even though they may have the best of intentions not to adopt more animals than they can properly take care of.

Over the years I have learned that all we ever need to know we can learn from rescue dogs. Dogs naturally have the qualities and traits that we spend a lifetime trying to develop. They don't need to invest millions of dollars consulting with therapists or purchasing self-help books, DVDs, or videos. They don't need to spend hours in seminars and classes. Here are just a few of the things I have learned from living with and observing my dogs:

- **Live every day with love and gratitude and be enthusiastic about the simple pleasures of life.** Dogs live in the now. They take time to stretch when they wake up and get plenty of rest and recreation.
- **You can learn a lot by observing and listening.** Dogs are focused and fully engaged.
- **Always remember that you are special.**
- **Be especially attentive to those you love.** Dogs stay loyal to the humans who love and care for them.
- **Approach life with strength, will, and tenacity.** Dogs know their priorities and live by them.
- **Be willing to change your opinion.** Dogs accept people unconditionally with no prejudices.
- **Always maintain your dignity and self-respect.**
- **Keep life simple.** Dogs keep their lives simple and express gratitude for basic things like food, treats, shelter, toys, and rides in the car. They do not multitask. They are not encumbered by e-mail, voice mail, or text messages. You will never see a dog texting while also engaged in a barking or howling discourse. They keep their meetings brief, with clear agendas.
- **Follow your heart.** Dogs show their true feelings and have no hidden agendas.
- **Always have a best friend and cherish that relationship.**

Dogs show their canine and human friends how they love and enjoy their companionship.

- **Don't worry. Be happy.** Dogs have no ego.
- **Make the most of where you are.** Dogs are authentic and easily integrate into their communities.
- **Follow your instincts.** Dogs are connected to nature and to their circadian rhythms.
- **Be adaptable and peaceful.** Dogs adapt and accept change, which is evident in the way they grow to love new people, learn a new name, and adjust to living in new environments.

All my dogs continually remind me that regardless of our beginning or background we *can* live a life of abundance.

In the first section of the book, I tell you about each of the dogs in the order that they arrived in my life. In the second section, I tell you about my special dog friends who have crossed over the Rainbow Bridge: Zach, Annie, Shasta, Kellye, Leo, and Daisy.

ZEEKE

"Why does Zeeke always position himself and his collection of
stuffed toys right where I am planning to vacuum next?"

MY GOLDEN RETRIEVER, Zeeke, is outrageous, overbearing, and needy in the most endearing way. (He is nudging my hand even as I write this.) He is my constant companion, shadowing me wherever his arthritic condition will allow him to go. He stays in the bathroom while I take a shower and get dressed, and he sleeps beside my bed every night. I have to be careful not to step on him whenever I get out of bed. If I don't greet him when I return home in a way he deems adequate, he uses his full body to block me from walking past until he has received the attention he desires.

Zeeke was not always this desirous of my attention. Here's the story of how we met and grew to love each other.

Early in September 1999, I had to take my cocker spaniel Gypsye to our veterinarian's office. That was when I learned the vet was fostering Zeeke, but I didn't know that he was available for adoption. Nor would I have considered adopting him because of Gypsye's condition—a senior with serious health issues—at that time.

I said goodbye to Gypsye not long after that vet visit on Labor Day, and after about a week I told my veterinarian I would take Zeeke as a companion for my collie Zach whom I will tell you about later in the book. I had seen Zeeke in his crate several times at her clinic, and I brought him home with it. That first night in his new home, however, he refused to get into his crate when it was time for bed. I had offered it to him because I thought he would want to sleep in it, but I didn't care whether he used it or not. The next day I put the crate in the garage and later gave it to a friend who needed a large crate.

Zeeke was very difficult. I consulted a trainer whom I knew to have a good reputation. After he evaluated Zeeke, he told me there was nothing he could do because Zeeke did not care what I thought and therefore would not behave to please me. This dog was very energetic and dragged me around the neighborhood whenever we went out for a walk. Part of the problem was probably just the contrast between my having just cared for a senior cocker spaniel and now adjusting to a young golden retriever. I was totally committed to keeping Zeeke, though. His energy and enthusiasm soon became one of the reasons I found him to be so special and why I love him so much.

Our favorite quote from the wall of our special room. (Author unknown.)

Everything began to change for us about two months after I adopted Zeeke. I had boarded him and Zach for a short period while I was traveling out of town. After I picked up the dogs, I think Zeeke realized he had a forever home. I hired the trainer to help Zeeke and me, and we learned enough to manage our walks and our life together in the house.

Zeeke has transformed into the perfect example of the typical golden retriever personality and temperament. Zeeke loves everybody and is always happy.

RESCUE TIP – Volunteer at a shelter: clean cages, take dogs for walks, play with the dogs, give them fresh water, and just spend time with them. Anything you can do to alleviate stress will help them present their best side when potential adopters visit.

When I got Zeeke, we lived in an area called Green Hills, which is an older urban neighborhood in Nashville. The yards are large with a lot of mature trees. A few of these older houses were torn down and replaced with new, larger homes. Our house was built in the 1940s. We walked in the neighborhood almost every evening, and Zeeke acted as if everyone out walking had come especially to see him.

For several years, I took Zeeke to Dog Day, a fundraising event for the Nashville Humane Association, and he always acted as if it were "Zeeke Day"—a term I use to describe his enthusiastic, positive reaction to any occasion where people pay attention to him. It could be people dropping by the farm to visit us or going for a checkup at the vet's or a bath at the dog boutique; no matter what, it is all about Zeeke!

For example, I take Zeeke to a chiropractor for adjustments. Somehow he knows the day we are going, and he wakes up excited. He loves to ride in the dogmobile, and the trip is about two hours long, so that gives him special time and attention.

The chiropractor is Dr. Sean Troutman, whose mother Jill manages the family practice and whose black lab Napoleon comes to work with him every day. I heard about them from Copyright Pet Resort where Zeeke, Hannah, Rocky, Ladye, and The Tramp go for baths. Dr. Troutman refuses to charge regardless of the number of treatments he gives Zeeke, his only regular, long-term pet patient. From the first day we walked in, Jill was smitten with Zeeke and gave him access to all areas except the treatment rooms. He also enjoys visiting with the staff and is always well behaved. Zeeke enthusiastically greets all of Dr. Troutman's patients, confident they have come to visit him rather than the chiropractor. Needless to say, a visit to Dr. Sean's is a "Zeeke Day."

Zeeke can no longer go for walks because of structural issues and arthritis in his hip. A few years ago he was evaluated for hip replacement, with the conclusion that he was not a good candidate. His regimen consists of liquid glucosamine drops in his food, a dose of Rimadyl, Glyco-Flex III, and shots of Adequan. Despite his pain, he jumps up and down in excitement for his food and medicine twice a day. Though this may not be the ideal behavior, I encourage him to break the rules. I feel it's important for him to move as much as possible. Plus, I find Zeeke's cheerfulness and focus on what he is able to do inspirational.

RESCUE TIP - Dogs in shelters are often scared because they have been taken out of the environment they are familiar with and placed in one that is unfamiliar. Anything you can do to help a shelter animal relax will make him more appealing to potential adopters. Carve out an hour from your schedule a couple of times a week to stop by your local shelter and walk a dog or two. The exercise will benefit both of you, and the dog will burn up some energy, which will calm him and increase his chances of finding a forever home.

One of Zeeke's favorite activities is playing with his stuffed toys and scattering them throughout the house, and he is rarely without a stuffed toy in his mouth. His love of stuffed toys is rivaled only by his love of shoes and socks. His placement of the toys is baffling, and I have given up trying to figure out his logic. He seems very determined to place the toys in a specific location, which is rarely the same place twice. I often step on a squeaky toy if I am walking around the house in the dark. Zeeke frequently puts several toys in a circle and then lies inside the circle.

Prior to vacuuming, I usually pick up his toys and put them in the dog room. He immediately goes to get them and places them throughout the house. If I vacuum and don't pick up his toys, he follows me around and appears to be guarding them.

When I buy him a new toy, I "hide" it somewhere where he can "discover" it rather than giving it directly to him. He enjoys this routine because it adds variety and a challenge to his day. Once he finds the toy, he decides whether to tear it up immediately or keep it. Surprisingly, Zeeke has some toys he has had for years. I find myself wondering how he decides which toys to tear up and which to keep. It's a mystery!

Zeeke began inspiring me in the summer of 2000. Zach died suddenly and unexpectedly on June 13, and Zeeke was inconsolable—even when lavished with attention and taken for rides. He was totally uninhibited in showing his sadness and loneliness. I, too, was devastated by Zach's passing and was not ready for another dog, but I thought that Zeeke was. I called Collie Rescue and we adopted Rocky on June 18.

When I took Rocky into the dog's play area in the basement to meet Zeeke, Zeeke began jumping up and down and turning in circles. He was joyful to have a companion. I was very touched and inspired by Zeeke's capacity to love Zach and Rocky and to accept the circumstances.

Zeeke has quickly accepted all the other dogs that have joined our household. He is always extremely excited to see Hannah and Rocky. He runs to greet them and play with the toys in their room. Whenever they come up the stairs they receive an exuberant welcome from Zeeke.

Zeeke now has the best of both worlds as the "only" dog in my bedroom at bedtime and the companion of Rocky and Hannah during most days. He also shares time with Ladye when we go outside. He continually inspires me with his affectionate personality, peaceful temperament, and zest for life.

Zeeke's enthusiastic approach to life causes me to smile whenever I think about how much he enjoys every day and how he shows it. I begin and end each day by expressing gratitude for the many blessings in my life, and Zeeke's presence helps me reinforce this practice. Zeeke is a role model for accepting physical limitations and still living an abundant life. I can only hope that I will accept the aging process and the limitations that may be involved as well as Zeeke has. He also serves as a reminder to me to maintain a positive attitude and interact with people with the assumption that their intentions are good.

LIFE LESSON:

Live every day with love and gratitude and be enthusiastic
about the simple pleasures of life.

ROCKY

Why do Zeeke and Rocky need more time for their morning
bathroom break on the days I am going to the office early?

ROCKY IS A SHELTIE-COLLIE mix with a sweet,
gentle disposition and a willingness to learn
and adapt. He is a wonderful companion to the other dogs
and to me.

Rocky was a stray that got picked up on a rural road by animal
control. He was placed in the local shelter, where he remained until
Collie Rescue adopted him.

Five days after Zach died on June 13, 2000, I called Collie Rescue to ask about any dog that would be a good companion for Zeeke.
The woman I spoke with suggested Rocky, and we made an appointment for her to bring Rocky to meet Zeeke and inspect our home.
When she led Rocky to our front door, he was shy, but Rocky's
introduction to Zeeke went very well, and she approved our home. I
immediately committed to adopt Rocky, and she left him with us.

When I adopted Rocky, he was thin and his fur was in poor condition. Collie Rescue had put him on medication for a tick disease. He was awkward and didn't seem to know what to do. He was also not socialized and was unsure how to act around other dogs.

RESCUE TIP – Volunteer with a rescue group: many groups rescue breed-specific full-breed/mixes, but others focus on special needs, older or younger animals, animals about to be euthanized, and so on. Find a rescue group that matches your interests (or start your own) and commit a few hours a week to helping the organization run more efficiently.

Rocky also did not know how to go up and down stairs to reach the heated and air-conditioned area we had renovated in the basement to accommodate the dogs. The first day at our house, I tried to get him to follow me to the basement, but he did not know what to do, so I carried Rocky down the stairs. I had to carry him up and down a few more times until he learned from watching Zeeke how to both climb and descend.

Unlike Zeeke, Hannah, Ladye, The Tramp, and Barney, Rocky had no formal education. Yet he has never gone to the bathroom in the house, and his demeanor is always perfect inside and outside. He learns by watching. It didn't take him long after observing Zeeke to learn how to manage the stairs, sit for treats, and walk on a leash. I think he is brilliant; I can actually see him processing information: He watches, realizes the steps necessary to do something, and then follows the steps he has observed to reach his goal.

My friend Emily and I say that Rocky is my perfect dog. He always comes when called and appears naturally peaceful and gentle; he is extremely well behaved in any environment. He gets along marvelously with Zeeke, and the two of them quickly bonded and moved into a routine that was similar to the one Zeeke and Zach had shared. At doorways, Rocky always waits for me to go in or out first. I did not teach him this, and he certainly did not learn it from Zeeke because Zeeke, in his enthusiasm, always insists on being first.

I call Rocky my "intellectual." This means he likes to tear up books. He has enlisted Hannah as his assistant. Since I think he is completely perfect, I ignore these breaches in conduct and clean up the pieces.

He is an avid gardener. When we lived in Green Hills, both Rocky and Zeeke often stayed outside in a fenced yard during the day. It was amazing what he excavated. I had to replace the large bushes he dug up with holly trees, but he also found those unacceptable for his garden—and promptly dug them up too!

Near the farmhouse, I have an area where I've planted flowers and landscaped. The dogs go there only when accompanied by a human escort. Rocky continues to help "water" the plants and inspect the flower beds. That works for both of us.

Hannah, Rocky, Zeeke, and me on the patio.

When Rocky gets into the materials to be recycled, I call him my "green" dog.

Rocky has learned to turn in circles like Zeeke when he is getting a treat or being petted and praised. By watching Hannah (who is not an ideal role model), his anxiety about storms and loud noises has increased. He has also learned from her to be impatient about being let into the house. I no longer leave him outside unless I can see or hear him to know when he wants to come inside. Recently I have noticed him observing how Hannah often has breakfast served to her in her crate or bed and I expect him to require the same service soon.

Rocky is something of a loner, usually preferring his bed in my closet to others throughout the house. He loves barking at the cows and critters and sometimes stays outside for hours. He is usually by himself and very focused on watching, smelling, and hearing whatever is around him.

Should I Take My Dog to a Trainer?

It's up to you to determine the amount of training you and your dog will need. I like my dogs to be generally well behaved, but I also want them to be able to just be dogs, somewhat free from the limiting restrictions we humans place on them. Many dogs that end up in shelters or with rescue groups have never been given the necessary attention, so they do not know what is expected of them.

An effective trainer will focus on helping you and your dog communicate with each other, making the classes as valuable for you as they are for your dog. Since well-behaved dogs usually have owners who are committed to making their relationship with the dog work, those dogs don't generally end up in shelters. For this reason, it is unlikely that your rescue dog has had any training. Research trainers in your area to find the one best suited for your needs. At a minimum, I advise you to enroll your dog in "basic training," where he or she will learn to sit, stay, and come on command.

Rocky has a bed in my home office and spends a lot of time with me when I am working at my desk there. When I say, "Want to go to work?" he goes to the office stairs. He usually sleeps on his bed and sometimes looks out the windows and barks. He is the ideal office mate. I have a screened-in porch adjacent to my bedroom. When weather permits, I turn off HVAC and open windows and the door leading to the screened-in porch. Of course there is a dog bed there and Rocky spends hours lying there. It is one of his favorite places.

Rocky about three years after he joined us.

He accepts that Zeeke and Hannah are the first to get attention from most people. This was a frequent occurrence when we walked in the evenings in Green Hills. Zeeke demands attention, and Hannah is so physically striking that Rocky is usually the last to be acknowledged.

Rocky learned from Hannah to go into a crate and frequently occupied hers. Now he has an open crate in their room. When I add a new dog bed in their room, I usually find him sleeping on it for the first few days.

Although he has no interest in toys, Rocky sometimes joins Hannah and Zeeke when they wrestle. He likes to go for rides and loves treats. And, even though he emulates some of the behavior of Zeeke and Hannah, Rocky is unique and has his own style.

An excellent communicator, Rocky is very direct and tells me when he wants attention. If he wants in or out, he barks. If I am reading and he wants attention, he barks and puts his front paw on the book. Regardless of what he is doing, if he hears me sneeze he comes quickly and is very attentive and anxious until I stop sneezing and assure him that I am okay. I have no explanation for his tender reaction and have never experienced this with any other dog.

Rocky usually will not begin eating until he has been rubbed all over and hugged in his favorite way. He was beginning to be stiff in the mornings, so I recently added a holistic supplement and liquid glucosamine to his food and he has improved. I use DGP, which is a joint support and revitalizer. The owner at Dizzy's Dog Wash and Corner Store told me about it when it first became available. Giving it to Zeeke delayed the need to start him on Rimadyl.

Rocky inspires me to be a more effective communicator, particularly in my role as a manager. Much of my time is spent in meetings with managers, agents, and staff; reading and responding to e-mail; and discussing issues on the phone. When people present information about challenges or problems, my natural instinct is to immediately propose a potential solution. Often, however, these individuals are not looking for a solution—they just want to be heard. In moments like those, Rocky serves as the per-

Rocky likes to be held like this before eating.

fect role model for me to improve my listening skills. It is a journey for me, and I am not there yet, but thinking about Rocky helps me focus on the person speaking and what he or she really needs.

Rocky's approach also helps me when people *are* looking for a solution or a decision. Even if I think I know what should be done, I make sure we have a consultative and collaborative discussion, with everybody involved "owning" the decision.

Rocky has also been a teacher and helped me be more observant of group dynamics. Thinking about how Rocky listens and watches makes me more aware of the body language people use to "say" things in addition to what they communicate with words. Rocky's gentle nature, modesty, humility, and intuitiveness—noble attributes to emulate—come from watching the other dogs and filtering the behaviors he notices in them through his own unique personality.

LIFE LESSON:

You can learn a lot by observing and listening.

LADYE AND THE TRAMP

*How does Ladye know how much rugs cost and always choose
the most expensive one to spit up on?*

*How did the Tramp's (and Hannah's and Rocky's) palate evolve
from street cuisine to a level of refinement that requires the
addition of canned food, baby food, or crumbled treats to their
natural premium kibble prior to finding it suitable for eating?*

LADYE AND THE TRAMP are the most committed canine couple I have ever known, and
they serve as an exemplary model for human
couples. Their devotion to each other is ultimately the reason
I am blessed to have them in my life and in my home. Just as
their relationship with one another continuously inspires me, their
behavior individually causes me to smile and laugh.

I heard about both dogs from our veterinarian at the time, Dr.
Kathy Kunkel. She told me that a compassionate gentleman had

picked them up on a rural highway and brought them to her clinic. An automobile had hit Ladye, and she was seriously injured. The Tramp stood over her limp body, guarding and comforting her. He probably saved her life. I initially got involved by helping cover Ladye's medical expenses. We agreed that when Ladye recuperated I would feature them in our company's weekly newspaper ad where we feature adoptable animals. (I began this practice in the early 1990s. The pets featured in our newspaper ad are usually from the Nashville Humane Association. We run a picture with specifics about the animals in need and list contact information for anyone interested in adopting.)

When Ladye and The Tramp were brought into the clinic, their fur was matted and flea and tick infested. They appeared to have been homeless for quite some time and were not socialized. Ladye had a broken jaw and a ruptured spleen, so it was a few weeks before the pair of dogs was ready to be considered for adoption.

We featured them in ads in two different issues of a widely circulated newspaper, both times with the stipulation that the two dogs would remain together. A few people wanted The Tramp, but no one wanted Ladye. We were adamant, however, about not separating the devoted pair. They continued to live at the clinic, and we continued to network to find them the right home. A client couple of the vet's took them for a trial visit and returned them in less than an hour.

RESCUE TIP – Sponsor a homeless pet. If you cannot adopt or foster a pet, you may consider sponsoring an animal. Funds you contribute could help offset/defray the expenses (shelter, food, medical) of keeping an animal in a rescue organization. This saves the organization money that it can then use to save other animals.

Good Girl/Good Boy Treats

When Zeeke would go into the house, The Tramp was aggressive toward him—twice with me and once with Geovanna. The Tramp was reprimanded for unacceptable behavior. In an effort to reinforce good behavior, I took The Tramp (often accompanied by Ladye and Barney) into the condo area for treats when he *did not* attack Zeeke. Now every time Zeeke comes into the house, the other three dogs run to get their "good girl/good boy" treats. The same thing happens when I am about to leave: Ladye, The Tramp, and Barney sit expectantly for their "good-bye" treats.

One weekend I had most of Saturday and Sunday unscheduled, so I decided to take Ladye and The Tramp home with me so they could play in a yard and have a break from being at the vet's office. Seeing them run together was like watching an artistic performance. I decided to keep them at my home for a few more days while we continued to try to find the right forever home for them.

I described my experience with them to the veterinarian saying things like, "Anybody who wants a companion would not get any attention from them because they are so devoted to each other" and "They just need someone who will provide for them and take care of them." As I was making those statements I realized that I could give them the kind of home they needed, but I did not act on it at that time.

After keeping them for a few more weeks, I finally made the decision to adopt them. I officially named them Ladye and The Tramp. I never considered any other name for either one, and those names have proven to be perfect for them. I chose the dogs and their names because of their appearance and their behavior;

I admit to being strongly influenced by the Disney movie of the same name.

I am curious about the past lives of all of my dogs, but I've been most curious about the history of Ladye and The Tramp. I wonder how Ladye and The Tramp got together and became so bonded. Are they siblings? Could she be his mother? Did they hook up on the road? Whatever happened to bring them into one another's life, they are a constant source of joy for me.

I think Ladye is a chow mix, although I saw a picture of a Swedish Lapphund in a dog reference book, and Ladye looks exactly like that except for the black on her tongue. She is petite with short legs and has the cutest face—small, with beady, intense eyes. She is almost always a lady. However, she's not very ladylike when she gobbles her food and would share The Tramp's if I were not there to distract her. Back when our front fence was not complete and the cows came into the front yard, she was also known to blissfully roll in fresh, very wet cow pies. I have also observed her "raising her leg" with The Tramp, Zeeke, and Barney. I tell her that even though she does not have ladylike manners all the time, she is *always* my Ladye.

The Tramp.

I think The Tramp is a terrier mix. He is extremely agile and runs faster—often leaping in the air—than any of the other dogs. In motion, he is beautiful to watch. He always looks disheveled—even after a bath or brushing. When I pet him, I call him Mr.

Tramp, which is something of an oxymoron considering that he's here to stay and would never stray from his Ladye.

Ladye and The Tramp almost always lie down next to each other, usually touching and sometimes letting their front paws inter-twine. The Tramp routinely cleans Ladye's face and ears and is very attentive. A few years ago Ladye had to have surgery, and The Tramp became sick while she was gone. I often look at Ladye and The Tramp when they don't know I am watching them, and they are

Ladye shortly after coming to live with us.

almost always wagging their tails—usually in unison. They con-tinually remind me to be happy and cheerful.

In preparing for Ladye and The Tramp's initial "weekend" visit, I bought a playpen for them and a bed for each. When I went down to feed them the morning after their first night in my home, I discovered that The Tramp had torn the beds completely apart. Thinking I had bought the wrong kind of beds, I replaced them with another style that appeared to be more durable. The following morning revealed a repeat of the previous night's destruction, so I switched to towels.

The Tramp didn't rip the towels to shreds; as it turned out, he had another purpose in mind for them. In those first days and weeks that they lived with me, it was not unusual to find The Tramp pushing a towel across the floor with his nose and chin in an effort to clean up Ladye's morning "toilet."

My friend Linda Burnsed, who owns The Farm at Natchez Trace, asked to have them stay there for a few days. She wanted the staff to practice boarding routines with Ladye and The Tramp in preparation for opening her state-of-the-art pet boarding facility. I forgot to tell Linda about The Tramp's delight in destroying bedding. Sure enough, he took a new, expensive bed and ripped it to shreds on the first night.

One of our favorite canine quotes has a painting of The Tramp on the wall of our special room. (Author unknown.)

Thinking I could outsmart him when we built the condos for Ladye, The Tramp, and Barney, we nailed the carpet in place so he would not be able to remove it. For some silly reason, however, and despite my previous experiences with The Tramp and beds, I bought some dog beds I found on sale and put one in each of the six dog condos that had been constructed. The next morning when I looked out my bedroom window, most of the beds were scattered all over the yard, disassembled pieces and stuffing everywhere!

RESCUE TIP – Begin an online newsletter that focuses on a particular rescue group and send out the newsletter to everyone you know. Update it frequently with photos of homeless pets, and encourage readers to donate their time and to contribute financially as much as possible to that rescue group.

A few months after adopting Ladye and The Tramp I took them to Cumberland Canine Training Center for obedience school. When owner Jim Molnar brought them back to my home and was demonstrating what they had learned and how to reinforce

Coming Home Routine

As soon as I drive into the garage and open the car door, Ladye and The Tramp (without ascertaining whether I am wearing a suit or jeans) place their front feet in my lap and begin a sniff inspection. My car is a Z3, which is low enough for them to climb into my lap, and it is kept in the garage near the dogs' condos. Ladye and The Tramp are particularly intent if I have been with other animals while away from home. Once they have completed their inspection, they give me lots of kisses and then go sit for their "coming home" treats. Sometimes Barney joins in greeting me, and he always sits with his best friends for treats. If I am driving the dogmobile (a Honda Element that I bought primarily because of the dogs), they wait for me to open the door in the garage that separates their condo area from where the dogmobile is kept, and then they run in and smell the tires—which have just driven through pastures and the barn area to get to our house—prior to getting their treats. The entire experience is a great delight to them and to me.

their training, he had Ladye go to her "place" and "stay." In her usual style, she made the most of the "center stage" attention and affection by slowly extended her front paws beyond the intended boundary. Jim, like The Tramp and me, had fallen under her spell and found it difficult to correct her.

For several years I bought annual memberships for Ladye and The Tramp to stay at the Cumberland Canine Training Center during the days I traveled, took vacations, and when I had evening commitments. Ladye and The Tramp won the hearts of Jim and Tammy Molnar and their son Jim and they always looked forward to their visits.

The Tramp dotes on Ladye and has developed an expectation that he should receive the same level of affection and attention from me. When we lived in Green Hills, for example, he would often lie limp on his back under the farthest tree in our yard when I called them to come in for the night. (This scene was also played out in the early morning hours when I took them out to the bathroom.) Despite all his "schooling," he adamantly refused to move. Of course I would eventually go out, pick him up, and carry him inside.

The Tramp and me
on the patio.

Ladye and The Tramp continually remind me that love is infinite. They are extremely affectionate with me now, too, and I have developed routines to give them the love and affection they want.

When I go out in the mornings, for instance, Ladye has to be held and petted. If I also pet The Tramp or Barney, she uses her paws to bring my full attention back to her. The Tramp lies on his back for his greeting.

Recently, The Tramp would not eat, so I hand fed him and sprinkled crumbs from treats on his food, which worked sometimes. I suspected this might be another "lesson" in training me to give him special attention, but I took him for a complete checkup—including blood work. Thankfully, he was fine and just letting me know he needed a little something extra. Now that something extra on his food is a routine. The Tramp also requires pets and kisses on his head before he'll eat.

Know What It Means to Commit to a Pet

Responsible dog ownership means that you make a commitment to your dog—almost as you would to a spouse or a child—to be a responsible companion. You must commit to the long haul, in sickness and in health, through the good times and the bad. You must make the best decisions for you and your dog, including keeping him healthy; seeking any necessary training and socializing; giving him plenty of exercise, healthy food, clean water, and plenty of attention until death do you part. Being a responsible dog owner means being considerate of others as well. You should always clean up after your pet, encourage him to be friendly, walk him on a leash except in leash-free areas, and make sure he is not a nuisance to people.

When I go into the garage to get into my car to leave, they expect "good-bye" treats and immediately sit. Ladye gets so excited that her front paws wiggle, and I say "Ladye bug dance," which causes her to become even more excited. Ladye loves to be held and falls asleep in my lap. When we are going into the garage, The Tramp and Barney enter through their doggy door, but Ladye waits for me to open the people door for her. Following is a copy of an article about this inseparable pair that appeared on August 7, 2003, in these Tennessee area newspapers: *Nashville Today, Green Hills News, Belle Meade News, West Meade News*, and *West Side News*.

The Tramp and Ladye have made room for Barney, and in many ways they've become a threesome. Barney and The Tramp spend lots of time together, and it appears to me that they often give each other the canine version of a high five as they begin a barking or howling session.

The real Ladye and The Tramp: A love story

Sharon Langford with Layde and Tramp

In the Walt Disney animated movie *The Lady and The Tramp* the pair of dogs act just like a romantically involved human couple, displaying the very human emotions of devotion and fidelity.

But that's just a movie, right?

"Wrong," Sharon Langford insists because she knows a real-life couple of canines that could star in a sequel to the film.

Langford, the general manager of Sharon Langford and Bob Parks Realty, explains:

The Ladye and The Tramp were abandoned on a rural highway and forced to scavenge for food until one morning The Ladye was struck by a car.

The Tramp stood guard over his companion, protecting her limp, injured body from being run over again. He refused to move until at last a Good Samaritan came along and took both dogs to the Little House Animal Hospital. There it was discovered that The Ladye had a broken jaw and a ruptured spleen.

Some six months later, Langford became involved, agreeing to help pay part of the medical expenses and to help find a home for them together.

"We advertised for two weeks in *The News*," she said. "Several people wanted to adopt The Tramp but no one wanted The Ladye. We were unwilling to separate them because of the bond between them."

And so the dog couple continued to live at the clinic, until Langford took them home for the weekend "so they could play in a yard." Or at least that was the plan— the dogs were "officially adopted" by Langford and never returned to the clinic.

That was in April, 2001. Today the dogs are healthy, happy and getting along well with the other three "rescued" dogs in the household.

The happiest of Hollywood endings would be for more people to realize the value of adopting pairs of dogs who have bonded rather than splitting up the "couples," Langford believes.

Story about Ladye and The Tramp.

Everything about Ladye proclaims I AM SPECIAL—her demeanor, her behavior, and her body language. The fact that Ladye knows she is special is a lesson telling me to take good care of myself and to believe that I am special regardless of how I might be treated by others. I have a lot of responsibility, what with taking care of the dogs, my house, and managing a large company. Ladye reminds me to "indulge" myself and balance all those responsibilities with experiences that make me feel good. I get massages, manicures, and pedicures regularly. I have leisurely lunches with friends, and I make sure to do other things that add pleasure to my life. She likewise reminds me that every human and every animal is unique and special.

The Tramp's devoted attention to Ladye is a constant reminder for me to be sure to demonstrate to the people in my life just how important they are to me. Since I have had The Tramp in my life, I am more aware of telling people—both in my personal life and in my role as a manager—that I love and value them and that they are special.

Together, Ladye and The Tramp are a constant reminder to me to love and be loved, to have fun, and to enjoy simple pleasures.

Ladye on the patio.

LADYE'S LIFE LESSON:

Always remember that you are special.

THE TRAMP'S LIFE LESSON:

Be especially attentive to those you love.

HANNAH

Why does Hannah drink water from plant saucers, birdbaths, and the pond when she always has fresh water in a clean bowl?

HANNAH HAS THE BROADEST range of emotions and behaviors of any dog I have ever known.

At her best, she has served as a pet therapist at a local nursing home; she has been named Champion Pet of the White County Fair; she has walked in the Mutt Strutt of the Nashville Humane Association; and she has spent days being calm, playful, and affectionate. Hannah would be named "Miss Congeniality" if we had an election among the dogs.

At her worst, she has broken out of her steel crate and stayed awake all night (with me holding her), frightened by thunderstorms or fireworks and trying to climb to an unknown destination, her eyes glazed and me unable to reach her. She has jumped into the bathtub, climbed into the clothes dryer, and tried to climb through windows and doors.

I don't know whether her behavior is a result of her DNA or life experiences—it's probably a combination of nature and nurture. I am also very indulgent and have spoiled her to help make up for the years of abuse and neglect she endured before coming to live with me.

Most of the time Hannah seems to have a relatively steady disposition, but that can change in an instant. For months after we moved to the farm, our friends Darryl and Blanchard continued to finish off details in the house and on the grounds and took care of the dogs while I was away. I explained to them that Hannah is not wired like most dogs, and that she might freak out in a split second. I was adamant that they keep her in her own room unless they were around her. Based on their experience with her, they didn't seem to really understand what I was saying (and why), but they agreed.

Hannah joined this canine family. (Left to right: Rocky, Annie, Gyngee, Zeeke, The Tramp, and Ladye.)

When I returned from a day in our offices that took me out of town, I learned that when Darryl had started a saw to cut stones for a flower bed, the noise had frightened Hannah so much that she had run at him and bit him before he could react. She bit through his work glove, puncturing his hand, and later she also bit him on his butt (with no injury) when he was pulling a ladder across the floor in her room. She is extremely sensitive and reactive to certain sounds.

I adopted Hannah, a collie, from the Nashville Humane Association for my mother, who had had a collie when she was a girl.
My mom had been so taken with Zach (you'll read about him
in the next section of this book) because he reminded her of her
childhood companion that she asked me to find a collie for her.
Her intention was that the rescued dog would live with her two
Great Pyrenees in a fenced yard bordering a cattle pasture. This
seemed like an ideal home for a collie.

No collies were available in Nashville when I began my search.
I inquired through Collie Rescue and was given information about
collies available in other states. I was considering that option
when I received a call that the Nashville Humane Association had
received a collie. The person who brought the dog to them did
not even know whether it was male or female and called the dog
Pointer because of its nose.

I picked the dog up and took her immediately to our vet. The
collie was infested with fleas, and the condition of her hair, which
had the texture of straw, was so bad that she had to be shaved. The
clinic gave the dog that we eventually named Hannah a thorough
medical examination. I was told that she was shy, but the staff at
the shelter was not aware of any other emotional issues.

My nieces Jordan and Raeanna and I later picked up Hannah
from the vet's clinic and drove the eighty-five miles to my mother's
home. From our first impressions, we thought the collie would be
fine. Yes, she was shy, but that was not unusual for rescue dogs
because they usually have been taken out of an environment they
are comfortable in (often with someone they trust) and placed in
an unfamiliar setting.

Mother kept Hannah on a screened porch for a few days to
help her get acclimated to her new surroundings. I called daily to
check on her. All seemed to being going well until one morning
Mother told me that Hannah had disappeared. She had put her in

the fenced area with the Pyrenees, and Hannah had climbed the fence and run away.

RESCUE TIP – Take in any stray dog you come across and create flyers that contain a photo and description of the dog, as well as your contact information. Post these "Found" flyers around your neighborhood, in your local shelters and rescue-group offices, veterinarians' offices, the post office, and local stores—anywhere there is a bulletin board and lots of foot traffic. Also post a photo and description on websites and in your newspaper. If you are unable to find the dog's owner, try everything possible to find the dog a home. If the dog has noticeable qualities of a breed, try to find a rescue group that focuses on finding that breed a forever home.

My sister Ruth and I spent the next day driving country roads looking for Hannah. I placed an ad in the local paper and on the radio offering a reward and spent most of several more days driving, searching empty buildings, and knocking on doors trying to find our special collie. I was obsessed with finding Hannah and tormented by thoughts of what she might be experiencing.

One friend who was trying to help me feel better suggested that Hannah was probably lying on a rug in someone's house, but I knew better. Neither her physical appearance nor her temperament would make this very probable.

I thought about Hannah constantly and sent mental messages to her that I was looking for her and would take care of her for the rest of her life once I found her. The odds were very much against us, but somehow I knew I would find her. A few days after Hannah had run away, I was at my office and the thought came to me to create and distribute flyers. I immediately asked Becky, who did our desktop publishing, to create flyers, and I spent the next day distributing them in parts of three counties.

One evening about a week later I received a call from a lady who had seen a flyer and thought that she had Hannah at her home. She agreed to keep her inside until I could come the next morning.

I went to a pet store and bought a large, open crate and placed it in my bedroom for Hannah. Ruth and I drove to the lady's home—which was quite a distance from our mother's home—the next morning. I never allowed myself to think that the dog might not be Hannah. She told me that Hannah had spent a few days in their barn then crashed through a screened door that led into the kitchen. Thereafter, the woman had kept Hannah inside.

When Ruth and I arrived, Hannah looked at me and came toward me as though she had been expecting me. I wondered if she was responding to the messages I had sent her. Even though we had spent very little time together, somehow she knew; dogs often know more and sense things very differently than we humans do. I believe this is because dogs are so much more in tune with nature. The lady said she'd heard of some people who had Hannah in the back of their truck and were trying to sell her, but when no one would buy her, they dumped her at a nearby lake.

Hannah.

Ruth and I took Hannah to Ruth's house, which was closer than mine. We bathed the collie, and then I took her home with me. I really did not need—or necessarily want—another dog, but

I felt fate had brought us together. It became apparent to all of us that my mother could not manage a dog like Hannah, and I was determined to ensure that she was taken care of for the rest of her life.

When we got to my house, this mistreated collie kept her tail tucked between her legs, as if it were glued to her stomach. It was several weeks before she raised it or wagged it. She was very melancholy, and despite having to depend on me for her needs, she didn't show very much interest in me—or anything or anyone. I had never had a dog that was so emotionally detached. It seemed as if Hannah's spirit had been broken, and I wasn't sure how to mend it.

Hannah barking in front of Ladye and The Tramp's and Barney's doghouse.

At the time, my office was just a ten-minute drive from the house, so I would come home to check on Hannah during the day. Carol Nichols, our advertising coordinator in the Green Hills office, became our pet nanny and took care of Hannah and the other dogs after I relocated to the corporate office about thirty minutes away.

From the beginning, Hannah was very challenging. She had many fears, erratic behaviors, and what seemed like unrelenting sadness. She barked a lot, and I was always concerned that she bothered our neighbors in our Green Hills neighborhood. Carol or I would give Hannah bark breaks—when we took her outside and let her bark all she wanted—during the day when the neighbors were at work. Often at the end of these bark breaks I would feel sad for Hannah because I knew she wanted to continue speaking her mind. I would tell her that when we moved to the farm she would be allowed to bark as much as she wanted—and she does.

RESCUE TIP – Changing a dog's name when you adopt her will give her a new identity and help her forget about her past and transition into her new life. My sister Ruth named Hannah, but I sometimes immediately know what to name a dog and sometimes wait a little while and base my choice on the dog's appearance or an aspect of the dog's behavior.

After several months we found a veterinarian who had a dog that once had suffered from the same extreme fear of loud noises, and he prescribed a strong sedative for Hannah. We routinely gave her the medicine if thunder was forecast and when fireworks were expected. She was still stressed, but the medicine helped calm her.

Eventually, Hannah began to run and play with The Tramp, the only other dog that does run and play. That was Hannah's first breakthrough in shedding her melancholy mood. It's always great to watch Hannah and The Tramp play together. Later, she also began a wrestling type of play in the house with Zeeke.

Hannah also began going on evening walks with Zeeke, Rocky, and me. Sometimes when we were walking, she would hear a door slam or some other loud noise and refuse to move in any direction except toward home. When she insisted on going home, I would take all three back to the house and leave her there while I took Zeeke and Rocky back to finish our walk.

When my job required me to travel out of town overnight and when I took vacations, Carol would stay at the house. She took care of all the dogs, but she stayed the night mainly to help Hannah relax. Not too long after Hannah came to live with me, my friend Linda Burnsed opened The Farm at Natchez Trace, a fabulous pet boarding facility. I took Hannah there because they offer twenty-four-hour care. Because she is a regular customer, they have her sedative and can give it to her whenever she needs it. Staff members are also available to sit with her during storms.

At the Green Hills house, Hannah had to stay in a crate during the day when I was not home. I hated this arrangement, but I felt there was no other option if I wanted to keep her. Her highly anxious state in reaction to noises caused her to claw at and climb doors and pace if I did not keep her in the crate. I vowed that once we moved to the farm Hannah would never be confined to a crate for safety again.

About three years later, in keeping with the promise I had made to myself, when we moved to the new house I didn't set up her crate. She spent the first few nights pacing and getting in and out of my bed. I couldn't calm her. I decided to set up the crate to see if the familiarity of it would help her relax. She slept throughout the night. Hannah probably felt as though her crate was the place she was supposed to be and sleeping in it was a routine that comforted her. It had become her safe place.

A Roger Caras quote and a painting of Hannah in our special room.

Hannah is very strong willed and, unlike the other dogs, will not come immediately when I call. Sometimes she doesn't come at all. If I take a leash she may just sit down and refuse to move. After seeing her so scared and pitiful and imagining what she may have experienced, I don't have the heart to correct her. The two of us would be a dog trainer's worst nightmare! Though Hannah sometimes has this stubborn streak, she usually does anything she's asked to do. Her groomer, Mandy, at Copyright Pet Resort has commented repeatedly on how Hannah does whatever she tells her to do and will let Mandy move her around in any way she wants.

Hannah has a good life now. She loves her "special" room downstairs. Often when I am staying at home all day and I bring Hannah and Rocky upstairs to be with me, Hannah wants to return to her special room. Her crate is down there (with the door removed), and she has a large area if she wants to move around.

Though Hannah usually refuses to go outside early in the morning and she always refuses if a storm is expected—I think she must be able to sense the barometric pressure—her bathroom habits in the house are impeccable.

I have discovered a way to rub her ears that causes her to totally relax and let out loud, long sighs. She often presents herself for ear rubs. She also loves to be brushed, but she doesn't position herself so that I will concentrate on her favorite spots as my other dogs do. She just lies there enjoying the moment. I take brushing Hannah as my opportunity to stretch and move into a variety of positions. Perhaps by lying still Hannah thinks she is helping me with my yoga lessons.

Hannah is becoming more and more loving and playful with me. Sometimes I think she plays with me like I am a dog—with the play bows and barking. She has also started prancing and strutting. I believe she knows that she is beautiful, and I tell her that she is my angel girl. It is such a joy to see her happy, proud, and playful, remembering how she behaved when she first came to us.

Hannah is very vocal. She loves running the fence and barking at the cows or at unknown (to me) objects in the woods. She enjoys looking out the windows and barking at cattle and wild animals as well as simply walking around the house barking for the sake of barking. I have learned not to make calls to people who don't know her if she is in the office because she may bark so much and so loud we can't have an effective conversation. Most of the managers know her or about her, and if she interrupts it is okay. I like to think that Hannah's barking is an expression of her happiness.

As sweet as she is, she is a bit mischievous. I have a miniature lighted log cabin that has been on the hearth in the great room since we moved here. Glued to the front porch of the cabin were furniture, a dog, and a water bowl. I would occasionally find one or two of these miniatures on the rug and was confused as to how they got there. Then one day as I was walking through the great room, I saw Hannah (with her long nose) meticulously removing the last piece.

Hannah is in excellent health now, and her coat is beautiful. I was so focused on all her issues that it's only recently that I have become aware of her striking physical appearance. People continually comment about her good looks. The residents at the nursing home call her Lassie and love to touch her hair. I think her appearance is the primary reason she won her Herding Class and Champion Pet at the White County Fair last fall. My niece Raeanna showed her and I walked behind so that I could help if Hannah did not walk according to the judge's instructions, but she was great. We were so proud of her!

Hannah and I share the characteristics of having a strong will and being tenacious. Neither of us could be where we are now without this philosophy toward life. Being aware that we share these traits probably helps me understand and accept her behavior and gives me the patience she requires. Hannah's strong will and tenacity are now more apparent than mine, but people who know me will comment about my determination and quiet strength. Hannah is a role model for knowing what you want and what you will and will not accept or do. She can also seem so fragile that my heart breaks for her, but she always rebounds and keeps getting better. Finding Hannah was a miracle, and it is a pleasure for me to take care of her—Hannah's way.

LIFE LESSON:

Approach life with strength, will, and tenacity.

BARNEY

Why are the flower beds in the front yard always on a direct route to where Barney and company are going?

MY EXPERIENCE WITH BARNEY causes me to ponder the relevance of Einstein's words about the importance of deciding whether we live in a friendly universe or an unfriendly one. Nowadays Barney behaves most of the time as if he were living in a friendly universe. It wasn't always that way, however, and his transition reminds me that when animals and humans act in a hostile and aggressive manner, such behavior is generally the result of fear, and we need to help them by extending love and tolerance.

Barney, a mix of two (or more) different kinds of hounds, was feral when I got him. He had a long and challenging journey to arrive at the state of equilibrium where he is now.

Barney came into my life in November 2004. One day at work I received a phone call from a teacher at an elementary school requesting help in removing two dogs that were hanging around the school. She knew I loved animals and she knew my real estate company's weekly newspaper ads featured adoptable pets. I called Carol, and we agreed to take food over to the school to investigate the situation after work. When we arrived, the dogs would not come close to us, and they behaved in a way that scared Carol. We put the food out for them and left.

Metropolitan Animal Control had already been contacted. They had placed traps in an effort to catch the dogs, but those efforts had been unsuccessful.

RESCUE TIP – Most shelters and rescue organizations spay or neuter dogs before they are adopted, but some shelters don't have the necessary funding. If you know of a shelter that does not spay or neuter the dogs before releasing them for adoption, offer to pay for the service. By reducing births, you will help reduce the number of animals that enter the shelter system.

After a few days of lingering near the school, one of the dogs wandered over to a nearby business, and the owner took pity on him and gave him food and shelter. I learned about that change in the situation one morning when I went to take food and water to both dogs and found one of them gone. The businessman and his wife had taken in the stray and were providing it with food and shelter at their house, which was adjacent to their business. Sadly, after staying with them for just a few days, the dog ran onto the highway and was fatally injured when struck by an automobile. It was somewhat comforting, though, to know that the dog had experienced some kindness.

Carol and I continued to take food and water to the second stray. We were unable to catch him, so I hired a mobile veterinarian who had dog-catching expertise. The veterinarian tried on two occasions, but could not catch the dog. The next week there was an ice storm, which made it impossible for us to drive to the school for two days. We worried constantly about the dog, which Carol had taken to calling Barney.

In January 2005, Metro caught Barney in a trap. They planned to euthanize him because they thought he was a vicious dog. Carol and I were determined to save him. We convinced Metro authorities to allow me to have a trainer come to the facility to give him a temperament test. The trainer, Tammy Molnar, was able to get a collar on Barney, and the temperament assessment she administered indicated that he was not an overly aggressive animal. I was permitted to adopt Barney by signing an agreement with more liability than the usual contract.

Tammy took Barney to Cumberland Canine Training Center, and he stayed there for several months. Our plan was to rehabilitate him and find him a permanent home. I visited him but did not try to bond with him because I did not want him to get attached

Barney's Front-yard Bio Break

Barney—along with his pals Ladye and The Tramp—is always exuberant about going to the front-yard area when we take Zeeke to the bathroom. They can only go there accompanied by a person. I marvel at their enthusiasm, and it inspires me to cherish enjoyable daily activities. In fact, they are as excited as I would be if I were leaving for an Alaskan cruise! The three dogs sit by the gate in expectation, and Barney usually makes whining noises. When the gate is opened, he, Ladye, and The Tramp bolt through and race down the driveway to the yard and run around smelling and marking the area. Their behavior is the same every time. They never lose their enthusiasm.

to me (or me to get attached to him). Tammy and her husband and business partner, Jim, gave me a reduced rate, and I had Barney neutered and given the medical attention he needed. I was very sad to learn that part of Barney's tail had been frostbitten during the ice storm and would need to be amputated.

After several months, Jim and Tammy told me that Barney was developing kennel syndrome and needed a different environ-

One of my visits with Barney at The Farm at Natchez Trace.

ment. My friend Linda Burnsed, who owns The Farm at Natchez Trace, volunteered to keep him there and did not charge me.

He did very well in that setting for several months. Barney's room had a window so he could see outside, and it was equipped with a TV. The Farm at Natchez Trace is staffed with very caring, compassionate people, and they were committed to helping Barney. There are several acres, a creek, and fenced areas where he could be off leash to move about freely and be more stimulated by the environment. But we all knew we needed to find someone who would adopt Barney. A few people who were interested in doing so and were willing to do the work necessary for a special needs dog came to visit, but when they approached his kennel Barney would lunge at the door and bark, scaring them away.

After several months, Barney began to regress. I hired a "voodoo lady," that is, an energy therapist who was recommended by a staff person at The Farm at Natchez Trace. She had several sessions with Barney and me and determined that he was bonded to me. I made a decision to focus on developing a relationship with Barney with the intention of taking him to live with us when we moved to the farm. At the time, the house was under construction and about six months away from completion.

I began visiting Barney regularly. He began to improve, but it was evident that he needed to be in a home environment. For several reasons I couldn't take him to my home in Green Hills. He was terrified of traffic, and my house there was in a heavily trafficked area, plus I already had five dogs. I didn't know what to do, so I asked around to see if anyone had any advice.

RESCUE TIP – Donate food, shampoo, leashes, collars, crates, toys, bedding, food/water dishes, treats, vet services, medicine, flea/tick prevention products, or anything else you think might be useful to your local rescue or shelter.

Bonnie, the night manager at The Farm at Natchez Trace, took Barney home with her after completing her shift. She offered to foster him until I could take him. She was his angel and his lifeline to a forever home. I visited Barney regularly during this time to maintain and strengthen the bond we had formed.

After I had moved to the farm and the fencing was almost complete, Linda and her managers had a management-planning seminar at my house. I asked them to bring Barney so that he could begin getting familiar with what would be his home. Barney was very scared and stayed with Bonnie the entire time. I was devastated because I had thought he would be interested in all the smells, seeing Ladye and The Tramp again (Bonnie had taken Barney to meet them when they were staying at The Farm at Natchez Trace during my move), and having a large new area to explore.

I thought about how Barney had acted and again wondered if I was doing the right thing for him. After a day or so I called Bonnie and shared my concerns, telling her that all I had ever wanted to do was help Barney. I told her that if he was so attached to her I did not want to take him away. I also told her that if she would keep him I would be financially responsible for whatever he needed. In the end, we agreed that I would be able to give him the best home because of the farm environment, and we scheduled the date when I would come pick him up.

When I brought Barney home, he was scared and trembling so violently when I turned off the motor that the vehicle was shaking. Darryl and Blanchard were finishing the house, and they began helping Barney adjust. During the months they worked on the farm, the two men helped Barney learn to trust people and how to use a doggy door they installed in the garage.

All the dogs accepted the addition of Barney into the family. Ladye and Hannah tried to play with him. Although Barney never actually played with them, he nevertheless quickly integrated with them.

Shortly after he came to live with us, Barney began to lose weight. Our veterinarian suggested I take Barney to the clinic for some blood work. Darryl helped me carry Barney to the dogmobile, that is, my Honda Element, and went with us. I call it that because I bought it for the dogs. I had a Jeep Wrangler but after Hannah joined us, I needed a vehicle to accommodate three large dogs. I was beginning to think about what to buy when I heard "Click and Clack" talking about a new vehicle Honda was introducing. I went to a dealership and learned that it was the Element. I liked that it had no carpet and the way the doors opened with a "safe" place in the rear for Hannah. Unlike when I first brought him home, Barney was okay during the ride to the clinic. But when I opened the car door and the roar of the traffic whooshed in, Barney became terrified and began to shake.

The blood tests revealed that there was nothing wrong with Barney. Lynn at Dizzy's Dog Wash and Corner Store recommended that I change his food to Pinnacle brand's trout and sweet potato mix. He was fine within a few weeks after switching his food.

Barney recently had a major breakthrough. I was repotting plants and needed to go a short distance on the farm to get some gravel. I invited Ladye and The Tramp, and they immediately jumped into the dogmobile. Barney seemed interested so I asked him if he wanted to go. He somewhat tentatively got in and was calm during the short trip. He'd come a long way—no pun intended—from needing to be lifted into a vehicle to go anywhere.

Providing for Your Dog

Before you bring a/another dog into your family, you should evaluate your circumstances to see if it makes sense for you and for the dog. Every dog owner comes up with standards for caring for their animal companion. Some owners feel the need to walk their dog several times a day; others are comfortable knowing their dog has a large backyard in which to run around. Some want to give their pup new experiences, so they take him on field trips and provide as much stimulation as possible.

One of the main reasons owners end up surrendering their pets to shelters is because they don't understand the responsibilities of raising an animal or the expenses of food and visits to the veterinarian. Although it is noble to want to save and take care of as many dogs as possible, be realistic and determine what you can really handle before adopting another dog.

Barney has been transformed from being an animal with major problems to being a healthy, affectionate, entertaining, and enjoyable companion. It's charming to watch him at mealtimes, for example. Even though he has had a dependable food supply for more than three years, he still can hardly wait until he is served each and every meal, and he seems to inhale his food. He sits for treats, comes when called, and presents himself to be petted by everyone he recognizes. He can spend hours barking at cattle.

All that barking, in fact, has earned Barney the most-respected bark award among his peers. (Hannah, on the other hand, would get the least-respected bark award because she barks so much that the others pay her little attention. Sandy's bark and Rusty's bark both have a lot of credibility.) If Barney barks and runs toward

Barney on the patio area leading to their condos.

the woods or pasture, most of the other dogs follow and participate in the barking because they know he's on to something good. About half the farm is bordered by woods, which provide lots of critter sounds, sights, and smells. The wild turkeys gobbling and the coyotes howling send the dogs into a frenzy.

Barney has the most melodious deep baritone howl—I even find it beautiful when his nighttime melodies awaken me. He has definitely evolved into the howling leader among my rescues. The Tramp tries to howl with him—but his howl is hilarious and more like an intermittent tenor. The Tramp's philosophy about howling is a frequent reminder that we should do what we enjoy doing—singing, playing musical instruments, painting, and so on—and never compare our performance to another's. If The Tramp were to compare the quality of his howling to Barney's, he would probably never howl again. The Tramp would miss the bliss of howling, and I would miss the fun of hearing and watching them.

Barney has become something of a caretaker for Ladye and, especially, The Tramp. He recently became my "hero" when he alerted me that Ladye and The Tramp had gotten out of the yard and into the pasture. Barney is very vocal, and it's not unusual to hear him barking. But there was something different about the sound this time. I looked out the window and saw that the cows had knocked the gates apart, which allowed Ladye and The Tramp access to the pasture. Darryl quickly repaired the gates and all dogs are now totally secure.

It's funny to watch Barney bark at The Tramp to get him out of the way when I drive into the garage or to beckon him to come into the garage for treats. It remains a mystery why he doesn't bark at Ladye.

Barney inspires me by his spirit and willingness to learn and grow. Barney is a constant reminder to me to be open-minded and to realize that the conclusions and assumptions I have made may be wrong. He helps me recognize when I have been mistaken and makes it easier for me to say I am sorry. Through his influence, I am trying to always be open and receptive to new information and to change.

There were times during the twenty-three months of care he received before he came to live with me that I wondered if I had made a mistake in going to such lengths to save him. Now when I see him sitting in the yard looking at "his land," I know it was the right decision for Barney. This is a perfect environment for him. It is such a joy to see him enjoying his life and continuing to be more trusting and loving, all the while giving back far more than he has received.

LIFE LESSON:

Be willing to change your opinion.

SANDY

Why does Sandy almost always jump in her pool
when we are taking pictures of her?

SANDY IS A MUTT, probably a Great Pyrenees mix, that my brother Samuel found and Geovanna rescued. One afternoon as I was leaving one of our Murfreesboro offices, I had a message to call Geovanna. She told me that when I got home, I would find a new dog in the separate fenced area on the driveway side of the house. Samuel had seen the dog in the same area of a cornfield for several consecutive days. It's likely that her original owners had dumped Sandy in the cornfield, and she was waiting there, hoping her owners would return.

We kept her separated from the other dogs until she had had a medical checkup and vaccinations. Sandy seemed very congenial, and I thought she would get along well with Ladye, The Tramp, and Barney. And she did—at first. During feeding, each dog focused on its own meal. But when we went out onto the patio, The

Tramp suddenly growled and lunged at Sandy. I got The Tramp to back off, but then Sandy became the aggressor and lunged at

Sandy getting out of the swimming pool.

The Tramp. It seemed that she wanted to be the boss. It was clear that this arrangement would not work. I immediately took her back to the separate fenced area, which became her home. Sandy has seemed at home here since the afternoon of her arrival. I kept her in a separate fenced area or in the unfinished part of the basement depending on the weather. She was fine with Zeeke, Hannah, and Rocky, but she sometimes irritated Rocky because she was so active and he wasn't interested in playing. After she recuperated from being spayed, I moved her to a separate area that had a connecting doghouse.

During the time she was staying in the basement, Geovanna and I would take her out in the front yard for potty breaks. There's a pond in the yard as a landscape feature, and sometimes Sandy would make a beeline for it and play in the water. But the pond is not intended as a swimming pool for dogs. I bought her a kiddie pool instead; Geovanna put it in her yard, and Sandy loves it.

I think Sandy is very intelligent and resourceful. She has the ability to hold on to two conflicting thoughts or emotions simultaneously, which I have read is a sign of intelligence. While she is eating she wags her tail and likes for me to rub and scratch her fur, but she growls and barks in a scolding manner if she thinks Rusty may be considering sharing her food.

Sandy is very energetic, and it became evident that she needed a playful, high-energy, submissive companion. For the first time in a very long time, I was actually thinking about adopting another dog that would be Sandy's companion, and that's when the universe sent us Rusty. He is perfect for her. They are both high energy and about the same size, and Rusty is comfortable with Sandy being the boss.

I love looking out my office window and watching them play. They spend hours chasing each other, wrestling, and barking toward the woods and at the cattle. Recently, Sandy was playing with a large stuffed toy and Rusty started barking in her face. After a minute or two she extended the toy to him, and they played tug-of-war for a few minutes and then discarded the toy and started chasing each other.

Sandy and Rusty have discovered (like Zeeke, Barney, and The Tramp) the bliss of removing the stuffing from toys. I had given Sandy a large ball, and she learned to retrieve it. After Rusty joined us, I would see the two of them running and playing with it. A few days ago I saw Sandy having great fun pulling out the stuffing.

Sometimes I see them with their heads together smelling the ground and gently pawing the dirt, then smelling again and pawing. They are probably doing research. They remind me to be curious about and interested in nature and to take time to play.

Sandy is increasingly affectionate and wraps her body around me. She has the sweetest face and smile and the longest legs. Sandy has the hair color—shades of blond and honey—that I (and probably a lot of other women) would happily pay a salon to have. Her tail is curled tightly, unlike any tail I have seen on a dog. Her coat is healthy now and she has gained weight. In fact, she reminds me of the dog in the musical *Annie*.

RESCUE TIP – Occasionally, shelters and rescue organizations have space and can take animals from other counties or states. Adopters often are interested in posts advertising dogs being put up for adoption that are hundreds of miles away. There may not be a rescue group in your area that focuses on an uncommon breed. One way you can help a rescue dog is to volunteer to drive it to its new family or to a rescue organization. Let your local shelter and rescue group know that you are available to help relocate a dog, and let them know the distance you can travel. After you deliver the dog, reward yourself with a mini-vacation and take your time getting home.

Sandy reminds me daily to live "from the inside" and that we should have high self-esteem and respect regardless of our circumstances. I think we all have an inner compass that can guide us to where we need to be. Sandy knows who she is and has retained her dignity and self-respect despite being homeless, apparently abandoned in a cornfield. She reminds me not to judge people or animals by their circumstances—that is not who they are—so I should treat all animals and people with respect. Sandy helps me stay focused on being authentic and knowing what I really want and how I want to live. Even though she was in poor physical condition when she and I first met, her spirit always remains intact. She has maintained her dignity and pride. A quick study, she now sits for treats and responds when I call her name. She has a good life now, and she adds joy to mine.

LIFE LESSON:

Always maintain your dignity and self-respect.

RUSTY

Why does Rusty—along with his friends Barney, Ladye, and The Tramp—find so many events and things to bark and howl at during the night and find the daytime hours conducive to sleeping?

RUSTY'S MANTRA SEEMS TO BE "Eat, play, get treats, get petted, sleep, repeat." He is a hound/hound mix that came to live with us this year. My niece Raeanna and I were driving by an area where the barns and equipment sheds are clustered when she said she thought she saw a dog lying beside a tractor. We went back and discovered a very thin, timid dog. We got food and water and a bed for him and placed them nearby in a covered area.

He was gone from that spot the next day when I went back to take him food and water. My brother Samuel thought he belonged to someone who had worked at our farm, but when we inquired, we could not find anyone who knew anything about him. He would sometimes come back and eat only to disappear again.

RESCUE TIP – Help out a pet's foster parent by helping to pay for some food, paying for vet expenses, driving the dog to the vet, or walking the dog. Anything you can do to help the fostering experience run more smoothly will benefit the dog and the foster parent.

I told Geovanna that the next time she saw him she should try to bring him home to be a companion to Sandy. A few days later she called to tell me that he was in the yard with Sandy. He had spent a week in the woods with some people who were cutting timber and had followed them out. They had been feeding him, and he had slept under a truck.

He was very thin, and he was covered with ticks. Geovanna took him to the vet to be examined, vaccinated, and neutered.

Rusty is no longer thin, but he still eats as though he is starving, and he is obsessed with food and treats. When he hears me in the garage preparing the dogs' food, he starts barking and leaps straight up off the ground several times. I am under no illusion that he is that excited to see me; I know it is all about the food. Because he eats faster than Sandy does, I have started sprinkling a handful of his food on the roofs of their houses so that Rusty will jump up there after finishing his food and leave Sandy to finish hers.

RESCUE TIP – Shelters always welcome donations of treats, rawhides, and dog toys. The dogs get bored and depressed sitting in the kennels all day. New tastes or something to chew on will occupy them for a while, taking their minds off of their situations.

Rusty has been with us for a short time so I don't know him as well as I do my other seven canine friends. Nevertheless, watching him is a reminder to me to schedule "playtime" and to take naps and rest more. He also reinforces the wisdom in my decision to move to the country and to adopt a simpler lifestyle. He learned his name quickly, and he sits for treats. He is very laid back and does not want the responsibility of being in charge (that's what makes him such a perfect fit for Sandy). Rusty inspires me with his love of the simple everyday pleasures of life and reminds me to be enthusiastic about a good meal and a good friend.

Rusty.

LIFE LESSON:
Keep life simple.

DOGS LIVE SHORT LIVES relative to humans. We would like to be with them for much longer and wonder why they leave us so soon. I think it takes dogs less time than us to accomplish their life purpose because of how they live. They already know what's important, but humans take a lot longer to acquire that wisdom.

I believe that when their time comes we need to give them the unconditional love they have given us. Sometimes it takes more love to let them go than to keep them. Motivated by love and our desire to keep our dogs safe, we keep our companions in our homes and enclosed in our fenced yards. They no longer have the option to do as their ancestors did and find a quiet secluded place for their passing.

Out of my selfish need to keep Daisy with me as long as possible, I waited longer than I should have to help her. I made a vow then to always let each canine companion go when it is his or her time. I believe that dogs can communicate to us that it is time to let them go. My experience with Gypsye reinforced this belief.

GYPSYE

To understand the significance of Gypsye's behavior requires knowing about her lifestyle and her temperament.

Gypsye was technically not a rescue—but almost. She was in a litter delivered by my next-door neighbor's blonde cocker spaniel, Angel. My neighbor was Japanese, and she was not very fluent in English, so she asked me to help her handle the responses she got to the newspaper ads she had placed to sell the puppies.

All the puppies were reserved quickly; my friend Kathy even took two. I came home one day and found the sweetest note from my neighbor asking me to take the one remaining puppy because the couple who had reserved that particular female had changed their minds. My neighbor even offered to help take care of the

Gypsye's first Christmas.

puppy in her home while I was at work. I had grown attached to the puppies, of course, while I interacted with the people who looked at and bought them, and I had also followed up to be sure the placements were successful.

I talked with my friend Rita about the offer and the reasons I should not do it, especially because I was just a few months into a new career in real estate sales. At one point, anticipating the logistics of caring for a puppy, I said something like, "She would just be a little gypsy." Then I laughed and said, "Well, I guess that will be her name."

Taking care of Gypsye was much more demanding than I ever anticipated it would be. In some ways, she helped prepare me for Hannah.

During her first year Gypsye often stayed next door with her mother Angel at my neighbor's house, and my friend Kathy frequently brought Gypsye's two sisters over for day play in our backyard. Sometimes I also took Gypsye to work with me, and a wonderful man I was dating at the time usually kept her on Sundays.

About a year after I got Gypsye, I adopted another cocker spaniel, Gyngee, so that Gypsye would have a companion. When we moved to Green Hills, Gyngee wanted to be outside but Gypsye adamantly refused to stay in the strange new yard. Gyngee had lived outside when I got her and did not like being indoors; Gypsye had stayed outside during the days and usually came inside at night.

When Gypsye was ten, she developed a problem with her vertebrae and was on prescription food for a gastrointestinal condition. She also developed pancreatitis, and our veterinarian did not think she would survive. Gypsye actually recovered after a few days.

Gypsye was never affectionate toward me until the experience of preparing to say goodbye, which strongly reinforced my belief in helping animals when it is their time. Even though she wasn't affectionate, she was very demanding of my time and attention—to the extent that she had to stay with our veterinarian whenever my nieces spent weekends with me. Gypsye did not like very many people and did not like other dogs after she became a senior citizen.

Our veterinarian said that Gypsye was the most neurotic dog she had ever known.

At that time, I lived about five to ten minutes from my office, so I checked on Gypsye several times a day. My friend and office manager, Pam Sidbury, would go during the day if I could not, and Pam stayed at the house whenever I was away overnight for a business or vacation trip.

In the last year of Gypsye's life, I made several appointments to have her put to sleep, but she would rebound and I would cancel the appointment. On Labor Day 1999, I spent most of the day out of town visiting my family. I had asked my friend Linda Burnsed to check on Gypsye. That evening Gypsye fell down as if

Gypsye's last day with me.

in a seizure or from a stroke and gave me a look that clearly told me it was time. Even though Gypsye could walk after the incident, I was sure that she was ready.

I called our veterinarian and asked her to come to the house and help relieve Gypsye's suffering. She instructed me to give her Valium (which had been prescribed for her previously) and said that she would come to the house in about an hour.

I told Gypsye what we were doing, and I know she understood. I carried her to the back patio so that I could sit with her, and she was uncharacteristically peaceful. Gypsye made motions that seemed to indicate she wanted to go into the front yard, so I led her around the house. It was as if she wanted to visit her familiar places one last time.

Most of the time, however, we just sat quietly together. Near the end of our time together, she raised her head and reached over and gave me a kiss. It was the only time she had ever done that, and I believe it was her way of thanking me for our time together.

When our veterinarian arrived at the house, I held Gypsye and her passing was very peaceful.

I don't know how much longer Gypsye would have lived. We had almost fourteen years together. I was not willing to risk her being alone and having another episode. Her act of affection reinforced for me that I did the right thing for her and that it was what she wanted.

The Rainbow Bridge

Just this side of Heaven is a place called Rainbow Bridge. When a pet dies, he or she goes to Rainbow Bridge, which is full of beautiful meadows and hills where all of our special friends can run and play together.

There is plenty of food, water, and sunshine, and our friends are warm and comfortable. All the animals that had been ill or old are restored to health and vigor there. Any that were hurt or maimed are made whole and strong again, just as we remember them in our dreams of days and times gone by.

The animals are happy and content, except for one small thing; they each miss someone very special, someone who had to be left behind. They all run and play in groups, but the day comes when one suddenly stops and looks into the distance. His bright eyes are intent. His eager body quivers. Suddenly he begins to run from the group, flying over the green grass, his legs carrying him faster and faster.

You have been spotted, and when you and your special friend finally meet one another again, you cling together in joyous reunion, never to be parted thereafter.

Happy kisses rain upon your face; your hands again caress the beloved head, and you look once more into the trusting eyes of your pet, so long gone from your life but never absent from your heart. Then, together, you cross the Rainbow Bridge.

—Anonymous

ZACH

I MET ZACH WHEN I TOOK TREATS to the Nashville Humane Association for the staff to hand out to the animals. From where I stood in the parking lot, I saw Zach, a large, older, rough collie. We met just a few days after my cocker spaniel Gypsye crossed over. I had not even considered getting another dog because I was still very emotional about Gypsye.

As I walked across the parking lot, I saw a woman I knew from our time together as volunteers for Saddle Up!—a therapeutic riding program for children with physical disabilities. She and I served as side walkers to help the children stay on the horses. Because she was also affiliated with the area's Collie Rescue, she and a Nashville Humane Association staff person were walking a collie and evaluating him for that rescue shelter. I asked if she was thinking about adopting the dog, and she told me she wasn't. I asked if she had someone lined up to adopt him, and she told me, "No."

I heard a voice I recognized as my own saying, "I'll take him." I had not planned to speak those words—they just came out. I truly believe it was Providence. I have never had another experience like that and never regretted saying those words. Zach was an incredible dog, and I am extremely blessed to have shared some time with him.

Maybe at some level we knew we were meant to be together although our time with one another would be short. The depth of our connection and familiarity with each other cannot be accounted for by the mere nine months—from mid-September to mid-June—that we had together.

I was told that Zach had been at Nashville's Metro Animal Care and Control facility and was taken from there by the Nashville Humane Association. Zach remained at the Nashville Humane Association for some time. That was all I ever knew about his past. After we were together for a while, I felt that he must have had a good home some time in his past because he was so well behaved and affectionate. It made me sad to think how horrible it would be to lose a dog like him. Perhaps, as with other people I've heard about, Zach's owners hadn't known how to look for him or stopped looking too soon when he became lost.

RESCUE TIP – Foster a dog. Most of the dogs that end up in shelters could become a loved and valued member of a family. The biggest obstacle is finding a family. Fostering a shelter animal will not only take the dog out of the stressful environment of the shelter but will also ensure that he or she is kept alive until a forever home can be found.

I took Zach directly from the Nashville Humane Association to our veterinarian for a medical exam. Zach looked so sad but so accepting when he was placed in a kennel at the clinic; I felt terrible. I told him that I would come and get him in a few days and hoped he understood. It was the veterinarian, actually, who named him because she thought he responded well when she called him Zach. I accepted her suggestion because of my trust in her.

When I returned to the vet's office to pick up Zach, I was so glad to see him, and it was clear that he was glad to see me. Again, I had the sense that although we had only spent a few minutes together, up to that point, it seemed as if we had known each other for a very long time.

My handsome collie was never confined to a kennel again after he came to live with me—he played in a fenced yard or in the house. I had contacted a fence company and arranged to have an aluminum fence (the kind that looks like wrought iron) installed around the perimeter of the front

Zach.

yard. They fenced a small area of the backyard too, so that Zeeke and Zach could go out of the house directly into their fenced yard to play. I also had a doghouse built so the two dogs would have a place to stay outside while the front fence was being installed.

I was the only person on our street with a fenced front yard, but because Annie and Gyngee's space encompassed most of the backyard that was my only option. It would not have been wise or kind to put any other dog in the yard with Annie.

Introducing Zeeke and Zach to one another was very easy, and they quickly became buddies. I didn't know whether Zach had ever been in a house, so I put him in the utility room the first night. He pushed the door open and came out, so I moved him and Zeeke to the basement, which was a large open area that could be heated and cooled. That night the basement became Zach and Zeeke's area. From then on, they slept there at night and, if the weather was nasty, they played there when I was not at home. Zach was completely house trained and much better behaved than Zeeke; I was glad for this handsome collie's influence on my golden retriever.

Zach and Zeeke.

We often walked early in the morning and almost always in the evenings. Zeeke and Zach became neighborhood favorites, and people often commented about how much they enjoyed being greeted by them at the front-yard fence as they walked by our house.

The first time the trainer came to work with Zeeke and me, Zach was with us in the yard. It was evident that Zach knew everything the trainer was trying to teach Zeeke and me. Zach would sit when the trainer told Zeeke to sit, and Zach knew the command to stay. He also knew how to walk on a leash.

The bond between Zach and Zeeke was immediate, and their relationship strengthened daily. They slept next to each other on orthopedic beds that my friend Linda Burnsed had bought because we both agreed they were the best *and* because they were large enough. The two dogs played with each other, and their favorite game was tug-of-war: I even saw Zach pull Zeeke across the floor a few times during these games.

Both Zach and Zeeke enjoyed rides in the Jeep, and I would often take them with me on short errands. Their favorite trips were to a local pet store where dogs were welcome. Not only did I feel

I was socializing them by taking them to places where there were other dogs, I also felt I was giving them adventures in places they had never been before. I felt it kept them curious and interested in the world.

From the beginning I was totally smitten with Zach. For the first few weeks after I brought Zach home, when people saw him they saw only an older dog with bare spots where I'd had to cut matted sections of fur out of his coat. When I looked at him, however, I saw a magnificent, regal collie. After several months of receiving nutritious food and top-notch grooming, Zach's coat filled in and began to shine.

Take Your Dog on Field Trips

Most dogs love field trips. It's pleasing to see the enjoyment in a dog's eyes and on her face when she realizes she's going for a ride in the car. Exposing your dog to new environments, objects, people, and other animals is a great way to socialize your dog and give her new things to think about. Try to get out of your neighborhood or the areas where you usually walk your dog. Many businesses are dog friendly, but you could also take your dog on trips to visit friends and family, a farmers market, leash-free and nonleash-free parks around your city, any nearby body of water, wooded areas, grassy fields, and so on. Each new adventure exposes your dog to new scents, smells, textures, wildlife, people, and activities such as jogging, swimming, and chasing sticks. Your dog's confidence will grow with each new adventure. A dog that is comfortable in many environments and around different types of people will be more secure and balanced, and more enjoyable to be around overall.

I think Zach's favorite activity of all, though, was lying on the couch with his head in my lap as I petted him. Our time on the couch was usually on weekends and in the evenings, and we both savored every moment.

One morning I went downstairs to feed Zeeke and Zach and to bring them upstairs, which was our daily routine. As I was preparing their food, I realized that something was wrong with Zach. Usually he and Zeeke stood right beside me waiting for their breakfasts. That morning Zach remained in his bed. When I touched him, he did not respond and seemed to be semiconscious. I ran upstairs, called our veterinarian, and asked her to come to the house.

While we waited I alternated between sitting beside him and going upstairs to call his condition in to the vet's office. I also called my friend Linda Burnsed to come and help me carry Zach upstairs.

Before Linda arrived, while I was on the phone with our vet's office, Zach came upstairs and collapsed. It was his final act of wanting to be with me. I covered him with a quilt to keep him warm and gently caressed him. He quickly slipped into unconsciousness. How he ever managed to get up the stairs is amazing and mysterious; I put it in the category of a miracle.

When our veterinarian arrived, Linda and I carried Zach to her van to take him to her clinic, and I sat with him. Linda stayed behind with Zeeke. I whispered to Zach that if he needed to go it was okay. I told him how much I loved him, and I continued to pet him. He died a few blocks from our house. We took Zach back home and showed him to Zeeke so that he would understand what had happened to his best friend.

The autopsy revealed that Zach had died from a ruptured malignant tumor on his spleen. If he had lived, he would have gotten very sick. I am thankful it happened this way so that Zach did not have to suffer and I could be with him in his final hours.

Our last evening together had been perfect and what we would have planned if we had known what the following morning would bring. The only thing I would have changed, if I could have, would have been to hold him all night. I had mowed Gyngee and Annie's yard, and Zach had barked at the lawn mower. He loved doing that. We had had dinner followed by our nightly neigh-borhood walk and then quality time together in the house before Zeeke and Zach went downstairs for bed.

Zach often crossed his front legs when lying down.

Zach's ashes and picture are in my office, placed where I can see them from my desk.

I frequently approach important decisions knowing that my head is saying one thing and my heart is saying something else. If I don't go with my heart, I know I will make a mistake. I have read several books about how men and women make decisions, and it seems that people ultimately make heart (emotional) decisions. If I had not followed my heart and adopted Zach, I would have missed so much. If I had made a head (rational) decision, the reasons not to adopt him would have prevailed. By following my heart, I had the wonderful experience of being with him about nine months.

Zach was also the reason I have the joy of Zeeke in my life and why I love collies so much. Indirectly Zach was the reason I have Rocky and Hannah. Even though Zeeke's and my heart were broken when Zach left us, I would not have missed this experience. All our time with him was incredibly special, and everything about him has inspired me.

LIFE LESSON:

Follow your heart.

ANNIE

ANNIE WAS A MIXED BREED. She weighed about 60 pounds and had long black hair that was highlighted with patches of brown and white.

Annie was a feral dog that lived in the Priest Lake neighborhood where I lived before moving to Green Hills. The Priest Lake neighborhood was surrounded by quite a lot of undeveloped land, and I guess Annie hunted and fed herself from smaller critters there. A neighbor told me that he thought someone had moved away and left Annie. I had no way to confirm that information; I had never seen anyone with Annie. I saw her occasionally, and she always came from the direction of the lake and seemed to stay in the nearby woods.

I had been aware of Annie for just over a year when I saw her in a neighbor's yard being mated. I made the decision then to make an effort to help her. I began putting treats in the front yard, and after a few weeks she would take them from my hand.

During the first few weeks after Annie and I met, she never let me touch her. I assumed she liked me and wanted to get to know me because she would always walk close behind me. Sometimes I thought she might nip my butt or leg, but she never showed any signs of aggression toward me; evidently, she just wanted a closer inspection. Perhaps Annie was evaluating me as her future caretaker.

By this time it was obvious that she was pregnant. I decided to get involved to keep her from adding to the unwanted dog population and to get her the medical care she appeared to need. I continued to work with her, and she began to trust me enough that I thought I could put a leash on her. I made an appointment with my veterinarian to come to our house. Our plan was to sedate Annie and take her to the clinic where she would be spayed and vaccinated.

We were successful in getting the leash and a muzzle on her, but Annie gave me a look that suggested I had betrayed her, and she fought viciously to get away. After the sedative had taken effect, the vet and I carried her to the van. At the clinic, the puppies were aborted and Annie was spayed. She was also given a complete physical and the immunizations she needed.

Gyngee and Annie in their yard.

After Annie had recuperated, I picked her up at the clinic and brought her back to my house to let her loose. I didn't know what else to do and thought that at least she could not get pregnant. I did not think she could adapt to being confined in a yard. She resumed her routine in the neighborhood and routinely visited my front yard. At that point, I had three cocker spaniels—Max, Gypsye, and Gyngee—that stayed in my fenced backyard. Though Gypsye was frequently inside with me, Max and Gyngee stayed outside most of the time.

Annie.

A week or two later, my next-door neighbor told me she was going to call animal control to pick up Annie. My neighbor was afraid Annie would bite her child when the child came into my front yard where Annie spent a lot of time napping or waiting for me to feed her. I knew Annie would be euthanized if she were picked up by animal control, so the only thing I could do to save her would be to find someone to adopt her.

I contacted another neighbor who had several adopted strays to see if she could take Annie, but she could not. I decided I would keep Annie until I could find someone to adopt her. At that point I was just calling her "the stray dog." I decided to name her Annie, probably because of the popular musical by that name.

My yard was divided into two sections: the back section where Max, Gypsye, and Gyngee usually stayed, and the front section, the part closest to the house, which was reserved for flowers and landscaping. I was afraid to put Annie in the yard with the other dogs, so I put her in the back section and moved Max, Gypsye, and Gyngee to the area intended for landscaping. Annie quickly learned to use the doggy door and seemed content with her new lifestyle until we moved about two years later.

Our new home in Green Hills had a much larger backyard, with large trees and lots of resident critters. Most of the backyard was fenced with rubber/vinyl-covered chain link so the dogs could see everything. I had a fence and gate placed across the middle of the yard to create two sections to separate Annie from Max and Gyngee. I had sheds built in the rear and bought an igloo-type doghouse for each dog, thinking that would be a more stimulating and enjoyable environment for them.

Within a day or so Annie got out. Our new neighborhood was a place where she absolutely had to be confined. The veterinarian advised me that because she had been a feral dog, I might have to have Annie euthanized if she continually broke out of the yard. I had an electronic fence installed and later added a wooden fence (with spacing so the dogs could see out) on the outside perimeter of the chain link fence.

After Max died in 1997 (about a year after we moved), Annie seemed determined to be with Gyngee and tore through the middle fence a few times. At first I was scared she might hurt Gyngee but soon realized that she just wanted to be with the little cocker spaniel. Gyngee was the only dog Annie liked, and Annie was wonderful with her. Gyngee would have followed Annie anywhere.

Before the reinforced wooden fence was installed, they got out twice. My cell phone number was on their collars, and someone caught Gyngee and called me when the two escaped the first time. Annie would not go to anyone, but Gyngee would. I was extremely lucky to get them back home. The second time, I received a call about Gyngee, and by the time I brought her home, Annie had already returned to the yard. I think Annie escaped just for the sport of it.

Annie made quick decisions about who she liked, and it was a short list. When the man came to measure and install the underground electronic fence system, for example, I took Annie on a leash into the backyard so he could work unencumbered in her area of the yard. She was ferocious toward him, and as a result, he forewarned the fence system's owner-trainer to expect a very bad dog.

When the owner-trainer arrived, however, Annie instantly took a liking to him. I think her street smarts led her to size up people and other dogs and helped her decide whether she should like them.

Annie learned to play "Happy Girl" with me, a game in which I would say "Happy Girl Annie" and she would run in circles and we would chase each other. I often saw her leaping in the air as though she could catch flying birds.

Annie was always tender and loving toward Gyngee. She had no food issues with her playmate, although I always stayed with them while they ate. Sometimes Gyngee would be in a deep sleep and I would tell Annie to "go get Gyngee," and she would wake her. They sometimes slept together in Annie's large igloo doghouse. The two had happy years together.

RESCUE TIP – The average life expectancy for North American dogs is almost thirteen years. There are many variables that factor into determining this average: small dogs usually live longer than large dogs; the amount of physical and psychological stress the dog experiences affects his or her life span; and if the owner has been attentive to the animal's health its chances for a long life increase. Though most people want puppies, think about all the years of enjoyment you could have with a middle-aged dog (or even a senior)!

During Gyngee's last few years, she developed a form of dementia that caused her to be disoriented, and she reversed day and night. We tried several medicines but nothing was effective long term. She would cry in the night, and I would go out and give her treats and hold her. This developed into a routine of feeding her breakfast in the early hours of the morning—anywhere between one o'clock and four o'clock—and Annie adapted to that new routine.

I don't think anyone else ever heard Gyngee, but the reticular formation in my head was acutely sensitive to and focused on her. Sometimes I would bring her inside but she was restless and anxious. Her comfort level was highest when she was outside with Annie. They were truly best friends. Gyngee had never really bonded with Max or Gypsye, and I think Annie had been by herself most of her life.

I took Gyngee to a clinic to be evaluated because her condition seemed to be getting worse. On the day she was scheduled to come home, I had planned to take the day off to stay with her, but the evening before I was to pick her up, I received a call from the clinic telling me that Gyngee was experiencing heart failure and that I should get there quickly to say good-bye. I had known she had an enlarged heart, but I did not expect this outcome. I'm grateful that I was able to be with Gyngee in her last minutes.

Annie, Gyngee, Zeeke, and me.

Afterward I went home and sat with Annie and told her what had happened. She never played "Happy Girl" again and seemed depressed. Thinking she might be like Zeeke and want another companion, I brought Hannah around to visit a few times. Annie was not interested and was even a little aggressive toward Hannah. Of course, Hannah could not have stayed outside, but I would have adopted another dog for Annie if she had shown the least interest in having a companion.

Annie seemed to grow old suddenly. She continued to eat but seemed unhappy. Within a few weeks she got out again. Thankfully, I was home and saw her. She was very willing to go back to her area when I opened the gate. I walked the fence several times and never could see how she could have gotten out. It seemed to have a metaphysical explanation, as though Annie were trying to tell me something.

That evening as I was walking Zeeke, Rocky, and Hannah, I was thinking about what to do with Annie. Suddenly I had an unexpected and strong impression that I should let her go. I remember exactly where I was standing when this thought came to me. I believe the message came from Annie.

I decided to take Annie for a complete checkup. She was diagnosed with large benign tumors, and surgery to remove them would have required her to wear an Elizabethan collar. Annie would have hated that collar! No other physical problems were diagnosed, so I knew it was her spirit that had communicated to me that she was ready to cross over the Rainbow Bridge. Annie was at least ten or eleven at the time because she and I had been together about nine years.

I decided to help Annie go to a place where there would be no fences. It was very difficult from a logical, practical viewpoint because she had no life-threatening or terminal condition. If I had not received her very own message I could not have done it. Our veterinarian placed a muzzle on Annie prior to giving the injection. I respected her need to do that, but it was hard to see. The Annie that Gyngee and I knew did not need to be muzzled. When I sat with Annie I whispered, "Go find Gyngee" and told her there would be "no more fences for Annie Girl." Gyngee's ashes and Annie's ashes sit next to each other in matching urns in my office.

A few days after Annie's passing, and without having consciously or deliberately planned it, I drove to our old neighborhood. As I approached the area where I had seen Annie mating and made the decision to get involved with her, I felt her spirit. It was strong and all around me. I went there again a few days later, but Annie's spirit had left.

Annie's strong will, spirit, pride, survival skills, tenacity, focus on priorities, and love of Gyngee were all characteristics that inspired me. I respect and admire each and every one of these traits and hope that I evidence them more in my own life. The most profound lesson Annie taught me is the importance of friendship. We are so busy sometimes that we may not "cherish" our friends as Annie did Gyngee. I hope that I can become as good a friend as Annie was to Gyngee. She was a role model for unconditional love for your best friend.

Annie wanted both worlds. Most of the time she liked the security of a home, but at times she wanted to be completely free. Sometimes I do too. I think we all do.

A few days after I said good-bye to Annie, there was a major fire at my next-door neighbor's house. Our houses were close together and had adjoining deep backyards. All of the commotion during and after the blaze would have totally traumatized Annie. For several months my neighbors used part of my backyard to park storage trailers, and there was a lot of noise and traffic during the reconstruction of their house. This further reinforced for me that the decision I had made about Annie was the right one, and I was thankful she was at peace.

LIFE LESSON:

Always have a best friend and cherish that relationship.

SHASTA

SHASTA WAS A WHITE MIXED BREED that came into my life when my mother told me during a phone conversation that they had a "white Daisy" at their house. Not knowing if the dog was male or female, I said its name would be Shasta. Shasta was actually a male so what I did to him was akin to Johnny Cash singing his song "A Boy Named Sue."

Shasta had been hit by an automobile but not seriously injured. My brother Samuel had picked him up and taken him to our parents' home. We knew nothing more about him, but when our mother said the dog looked like Daisy (except that he or she was white), that was all I needed to know.

On the way home Shasta got carsick. Despite that mild trauma, his introduction to Daisy and Leo went well, and he quickly adjusted to his new home. I thought he had been homeless for a long time judging by his appearance when we met. I took him to be neutered and thoroughly groomed. He soon settled into a routine with Daisy and Leo, even learning quickly to enter and exit through a doggy door.

Shasta was very laid back and calm. The only time I ever saw him in a bad mood was in his senior years, after Daisy and Leo were gone, when Max joined our household. After his introduction to Max, Shasta jumped up on the couch, turned his face to the wall, and growled.

Shasta adjusted, with no further carsickness, to short rides to the veterinarian and to the groomer for baths. He quickly transitioned his quarters from the garage to the large doghouse after Kellye joined us. I think he played a major role in Kellye's adjustment and satisfaction in her new home. He was tolerant of Leo, who was challenging to both of us at times. After Daisy was gone, it seemed as though Shasta tried to be sensitive and comforting to me. He learned to walk on a leash when we left the yard. He had house privileges but stayed outside most of the time and always at night.

Shasta.

RESCUE TIP – Giving treats to your dogs before you leave them at home—alone or under someone else's care—helps take their minds off your absence. It also helps prevent anxiety and calm them. You'll begin to think that sometimes they actually look forward to you leaving—just so they can get those treats!

I never tried to teach Shasta very much because he knew what he needed to know to live the way he did. He enjoyed treats and toys and was always pleasant with people. Overall, Shasta was probably the easiest dog I have ever adopted. He had no health issues (except an albino nose, and we used sunscreen for that) until his last days.

Shasta was with us about eleven years, and all of that time with him was good. At the end of his life, he stopped eating and was very lethargic. Our veterinarian did not have a diagnosis or a solution. By that time Shasta had probably exceeded his life expectancy. I thought it was his time and decided the best I could do for him was to help him. His passing was as gentle and as peaceful as his life had been. I placed his best friend Kellye's ashes in his casket and buried the two of them in the family cemetery on the farm where I live.

Shasta inspired me by his contentment, peacefulness, congeniality, tolerance, and enjoyment of a simple, routine life. Shasta's "Don't Worry, Be Happy" approach to life has served as an inspiration for me to focus on what I can control and not spend time worrying about the situations I can't. Shasta had reasons to worry—he had been homeless and injured, after all—but he maintained a positive, happy approach to life. Thinking about how Shasta lived helps me keep an optimistic attitude regardless of the circumstances. It's a reminder that happiness is a decision we make.

LIFE LESSON:

Don't worry. Be happy.

Shasta barking.

KELLYE

KELLYE WAS AN IRISH SETTER that I adopted when she was a senior. She had been with one family since she was a puppy, but the family was moving from a house to a condominium and had decided they could not take Kellye with them. A mutual friend told me that they were considering turning Kellye loose in the country or having her euthanized, and she had told them that I would probably take her. When I heard about Kellye's circumstances, I immediately agreed to take her into our canine family of Max and Shasta.

We arranged for the family to take her to a veterinarian's clinic where I then picked her up and took her to my home. Kellye was a very peaceful and dignified animal. To my utter surprise, however, she immediately climbed over the 5-foot-high picket fence that enclosed our yard and that had been adequate for restraining Daisy, Leo, and Shasta.

I kept Kellye in the house except for walks on a leash until I could get a 6-foot-high fence installed. I also bought a large storage building to place in the yard: I had it insulated and a large doggy door installed. I had never had a large dog before taking in Kellye, and the doggie door into the garage was too small for her.

RESCUE TIP - If you know someone who is considering euthanizing their dog or giving it to a shelter, tell them about existing programs that will help them find another home for their pet. You'll probably have to do the research for them. Contact your veterinarian, local shelter, and rescue groups and ask about a program that serves as an alternative to shelter surrender. Buying the animal and the family more time could help save the animal's life.

Kellye particularly liked Shasta. She ate well and was congenial with all people and other dogs.

One day I noticed bright red blood around her rectal area and took her to our veterinarian. She was diagnosed with colorectal cancer and underwent surgery. She stayed at the clinic for a few days and seemed happy to see me when I visited. She had to wear an Elizabethan collar for a few days after she came home and was able to manipulate it to go in and out of her doggy door. She recovered quickly and resumed her regular diet and normal routine.

Kellye and Shasta with their Christmas stockings.

Within a few months I saw blood again, and again I took her to our veterinarian. The cancer had returned, and Kellye had surgery again. When I visited her at the clinic she seemed depressed. Her recovery from this surgery was not as quick as it had been the first time.

A few months later a friend of mine was at my house and called me at work to tell me that Kellye was bleeding. I went home and took her to the veterinarian who told me that the cancer had returned. I was unwilling to subject Kellye to a third surgery. It had been a struggle for her to come out of her depression following her second surgery, and it had been hard to see her mood changes since then.

I could not let her continue as she was, so I decided it was time to say good-bye. As I reflected on our brief time together, I was grateful that I had had the opportunity to help her during the end of her life. We had shared a Christmas, and she seemed to like her stocking. I know she had good food and medical care, and she had made a canine friend in Shasta.

I stood with Kellye and stroked her head as she crossed over. It was peaceful and quick. Because I had not prepared for this I had her cremated—the first dog I had ever requested that for. I kept her ashes until we said good-bye to Shasta. At that time I placed Kellye's ashes in Shasta's coffin and buried them together.

RESCUE TIP – Make a commitment to a shelter dog that you will get him out of the shelter to a forever home. Take photographs of him and spread the word. In addition to posting flyers and reaching people through e-mailing and posting on social media sites such as Facebook and My-Space, you might consider paying for an ad in your local newspaper.

Kellye inspired me with her gentle disposition and ability to adjust to a new home after having spent her entire life with one family. She was a good, well-behaved dog, content and engaged and easy to love. In fact she was my sister's favorite of the dogs that shared my life at that time. She rode well in the car, walked on a leash, and had excellent manners in the house. I was very touched and inspired that she could accept such a drastic change so late in her life and make the best of it. She was quite special!

Kellye was a wonderful role model for making the most of where you are. I have found myself in situations where I had not planned to be and did not want to be. Reflecting on how Kellye made the most of circumstances beyond her control helps me remember to look for the gift in what seems to be an adverse situation and to believe in a positive outcome.

LIFE LESSON:

Make the most of where you are.

LEO WAS A GORGEOUS blond cocker spaniel that I found on the side of I-40 near Knoxville. His instinct for survival must have kept him there until someone came to rescue him. There were no neighborhoods near that part of the interstate, and I have always wondered what circumstances led him to be in that situation.

I picked him up and took him home with me, which was about a three-hour drive. He easily came to me and was a good passenger.

Introducing Leo to Daisy went well.

I called the Knoxville-area newspapers to inquire whether any ads had been placed for a missing cocker spaniel. There weren't any. This was years before the advent of websites devoted to helping people find missing pets. When I could not find Leo's owner, I decided to become a two-dog household.

Leo was very comfortable inside the house but was always somewhat detached. I wondered if he might have been a show dog. He was well behaved at the veterinarian clinic and during visits to the groomer. His coat was in good condition, and he had the appearance of having been well cared for. I think he had been on the side of the road only a short time before I picked him up.

Leo had a funny habit that I have never witnessed in any other dog. He would catch a frog, hold it in his mouth, and bring it into the house. He did this several times, never once injuring the frog. His instinctual curiosity was interesting to me. The fact that he never hurt the frogs was evidence of his natural reverence for life and his fellow creatures.

While I was loading dirty dishes into the dishwasher, Leo loved to sit on the open door and "lick the platters clean." He just started staying with me in the kitchen, and I let him lick spoons. It soon became a habit, so I intentionally left the dishwasher door open for him.

Leo loved to help wash dishes.

Leo could also be very reactionary. If dogs have tempers, he probably did. After Shasta joined us, Leo would sometimes bite his nose. I have a scar on my nose as a result of one of Leo's bites. I had been playing with him, and he got excited and bit my nose. He was not angry or aggressive—just excitable. Thinking about his frog collection, maybe Leo just had a thing about noses.

Leo was an inside/outside dog and quickly mastered the doggy door. He liked to go for rides and enjoyed attention from my family and friends. From what I saw, Leo seemed to genuinely enjoy the companionship of Shasta and Daisy.

RESCUE TIP – Work out a deal with an obedience trainer and pay for obedience classes for a rescue dog. A well-behaved dog has a better chance of being adopted than one that would require more energy and attention.

During the last few weeks of his life, Leo lived with my friend Kathy. I made this arrangement because Leo had growled at Daisy once after she had gone blind and was near the end of her life. I was not willing to have her endangered or treated like that, and Kathy volunteered to keep Leo for me. He had always been her favorite, and because she did not have a dog, we didn't have to worry about Leo's moodiness affecting any other canines. She lived just a few minutes away so I could visit him often. Leo seemed very content with her. My brother Jack brought a very nice doghouse and fenced an area in Kathy's yard for Leo who was also an inside/outside dog with Kathy.

One night Kathy called me and said that something was wrong with Leo, and we decided to take him to an emergency clinic. He died within a few minutes, even before we could get there. I had thought, and our veterinarian agreed, that Leo was between one and three years old when he joined us, and he had been part of our family for almost seven years. I did not ask to have an autopsy performed, but our veterinarian speculated that Leo had had a stroke or a heart attack.

I had already bought a casket for Daisy because I knew she was near the end of her life. Kathy and I placed Leo and a toy frog in the casket and buried him in the family cemetery. He was the first dog to be buried there.

Pet Burial

It is difficult to think about the passing of a beloved pet. But with so many options available for final care of a pet's remains, it is worth thinking about before you are forced to make a hasty decision you may later regret.

Pet cemetery: Many large cities have pet cemeteries, and some veterinarians operate their own. Pet cemeteries usually offer a wide variety of burial options, including private or communal plot burials and cremation. To learn more, call the International Association of Pet Cemeteries and Crematories at 518-594-3000.

Home burial: If you plan to remain where you live for many years, home burial may be the perfect option for you. You should consult your local government; some cities and counties prohibit home burial of pets. If you are permitted to bury on your property, be sure to bury your pet at least 3 feet underground so that other animals do not disturb him and he does not become a health hazard.

Cremation: During the last couple of decades, cremation has become a very popular choice among bereaved pet owners. This is a practical solution for people who move frequently, do not have the option for home burial, or want to keep the ashes nearby or scatter them at meaningful locations. Some crematoriums perform mass cremations and then divide the ashes. When researching a crematorium, ask if they provide single cremations.

Leo's passing was totally unexpected. He had never been sick during the time we were together. I was trying to prepare for saying good-bye to Daisy. Losing both Leo and Daisy within a ten-day period was very hard. I also felt awful for my friend Kathy because she had gotten even more attached to Leo while he was living with her.

Leo inspired me by following his natural instincts for survival and curiosity. I particularly admired his kindness toward the frogs and his tenacity.

Leo's life reinforced for me what we all know—that we should follow our instincts. I think that is what kept him on the side of the interstate and allowed him to trust me enough to come to me so that he could be rescued and survive a bad situation. We all have natural survival instincts, and we need to be aware of and act on them. This is especially true when we find ourselves in a dangerous situation, whether emotional or physical.

LIFE LESSON:

Follow your instincts.

DAISY

DAISY WAS UNIQUE in my life and was the inspiration behind my journey with the rescues. I had more time with her—about fourteen years—than with any other dog, sharing some of my most carefree years and the worst experience of my life when my brother Ray was piloting a plane and had a fatal crash. During most of the time Daisy and I were together, I was teaching at a university and had shorter workdays and a lot of holidays, breaks, and vacation time, so we had more time together on a daily basis. It was just Daisy and me for several years, so I know the joy and contentment that can arise from a one-on-one relationship between a person and a dog.

I met Daisy when my husband (at that time) and I made a spontaneous visit to the Nashville Humane Association. It was providential! We already had a German shepherd, which he had adopted from the association and which was really *his* dog. We had not talked about getting another dog, but once I saw Daisy, I suggested we adopt her.

A medium-sized, mostly black dog with long hair and a slightly wagging tail, something about her resonated with me. When I inquired about her, I was told that she would be euthanized if she were not adopted within two days. This was in 1970. The next day she was in our home. I immediately named her Daisy, never considering any other names.

When we took her to the veterinarian for a checkup, we learned that she was pregnant. Daisy delivered the puppies in our utility room. Apparently, several fathers had been involved based on the puppies' appearances and on what the veterinarian said. It was during the birthing process that I fell madly in love with Daisy. We found good homes for the puppies, and as soon as she had recovered, Daisy was spayed.

Daisy was always so easy to be with. She was congenial with all creatures and humans. She had the qualities that spiritual teachers attribute to enlightened beings. She was playful and adaptable to any circumstance.

I basically allowed Daisy to do whatever she wanted, and she did not abuse my trust. There was no place in my life or home that was off-limits to Daisy.

RESCUE TIP – When writing your will, consider bequeathing some of your money to rescue groups and nonprofits that focus on animal welfare.

About a year after Daisy joined us, my husband accepted a promotion and transfer to Dallas, Texas. I stayed in Nashville a few months to sell our house and finish the academic year. After our house was sold and the furnishings moved to the house we had purchased in Dallas, Daisy and I stayed with friends. She easily made the transition to living in new environments even during the times I was at work.

Daisy was a perfect passenger and companion during our trip from Nashville to Dallas. She adjusted immediately to yet another home. I had accepted a posi-tion with a large, well-known pharmaceutical company and would be its first female rep in the Southeast. People who had recruited at the university where I taught during the com-pany's nationwide search signed me, but the local sales manager was not excited about having a female rep. In response, he reor-ganized the territories to give me the largest and most dif-ficult areas—including Dallas,

Daisy.

Longview, Tyler, and Oak Cliff in the Southeast region—which required me to travel three weeks out of every five. I routinely left early Monday morning and returned Friday evening. Most aspects of the job were challenging because of the logistics and the attitudes of some physicians and pharmacists toward a female rep. Added to that stress and pressure, being away from Daisy that much was agony.

After a few months I resigned and accepted a position as a regional manager for a cosmetics company. I could work from a home office and was not required to travel overnight. During the year that Daisy and I lived in Dallas, we made several trips to Ten-nessee to visit my sister in Memphis and my parents and brothers in Sparta. Daisy enjoyed each of those rides, and she was always content in whatever home or place we visited.

RESCUE TIP – Animal rescue organizations are always in need of funding. Have a fundraiser/pledge drive to benefit a rescue group or shelter. A short, clear message with a few photographs e-mailed to friends and posted on social media sites such as Facebook and MySpace could raise several hundred dollars with minimal effort.

Daisy was always very kind. While we were living in Dallas, a friend gave us two kittens, and Daisy would allow them to lie on her hair and snuggle with her. One time I was very sick for a few days and had to stay in bed. Rather than following her usual practice of going outside several times a day, she stayed very still and quiet on the bed with me and only indicated a need to go out for bathroom breaks.

After about a year in Dallas, I decided to move back to Nashville. I found an apartment and secured a teaching position at the university where I had taught before. I found good homes for the cats because they could not have played outside in Nashville the way they had in our fenced-in backyard in Texas, and I knew that I could not give them the home environment they needed, so I placed them with people who could. Daisy immediately adjusted to the Nashville apartment lifestyle even while I was away. We became friends with a couple who lived in the complex and whose door we always passed when going out for a walk or a ride. Daisy delighted in visiting with them and eating their cat's food.

One day when Daisy and I were walking she ran into the woods and did not come when I called her. Even though I considered her to be perfect, she did have "selective" hearing. Several hours passed, and I grew very anxious. When she finally returned, her fur was totally covered with barbed green sticktights. The groomer thought the only solution would be to shave Daisy completely, but eventually, with lots of time and patience, she was able to remove all of them.

At home one day during the end-of-semester Christmas break, a man wearing a maintenance uniform knocked on our door and said he had to check the bathroom plumbing. When I showed him to the bathroom he said, "Don't scream or I will kill you." I saw in the mirror that he had a pistol pointed at my head. He made me fasten Daisy outside my bedroom, and he proceeded to rape, assault, and rob me. I thought it very possible that he would shoot me. When he didn't and then opened the bedroom door, I was terrified that he would shoot Daisy. When I heard the outside door close, I ran and locked it and held Daisy for a long time. My fear that he would kill Daisy was the worst part of the ordeal.

Understandably, I was afraid to stay in the apartment after that because I did not know who my assailant was and whether he would return. Daisy and I stayed with friends until I could find another apartment. After that experience, Daisy seemed anxious when she saw any man in uniform. That was the only circumstance in which Daisy was not totally calm and laid back.

Our late brother, Ray, brushing Daisy.

When we moved to another apartment and met new people, it was a nonevent for Daisy. She was incredibly flexible and adaptable. After about a year we moved again to a larger apartment, and Daisy immediately adjusted to another new environment, people, and dogs. Our final move together was to a house that I had bought. I had the backyard fenced and a doggy door installed so Daisy could stay outside or in the garage if she wanted. We lived there more than eight years together.

During those years, I had a very active social life, having friends come and go and taking vacation trips. My brothers Ray and Samuel stayed with us during part of the time while they attended a nearby university, and their friends visited now and then. Daisy loved the company.

Likewise Daisy stayed with my brothers in their apartments sometimes when I traveled, and she also stayed with a male friend of mine. She and I traveled to Memphis several times to visit my sister, and Daisy was always comfortable no matter where we were.

Daisy went almost everywhere I went. She loved to stand in my lap and stick her head out the window while riding in the car. If a man I dated was not smitten with Daisy and not enthusiastic about sharing the couch with her, it was a very short-lived relationship.

Once I went to Florida for a week, and a friend took care of Daisy at our house. When I returned, Daisy's hair was coming out in large handfuls. I took her to the vet, and he said the symptoms looked like mange, but the tests were negative. She continued to lose her hair, and she had grown lethargic. He tested her again, and again the test came back negative with no indication of mange or any disease whatsoever.

A day or so after the last round of testing, I came home from work and found Daisy in a fetal position in a laundry basket. I took her back to the veterinarian, and he ran still more tests. Suddenly, I heard him yell from the lab. He was so excited; finally the tests showed that Daisy did, indeed, have mange. We had no idea how she could have contracted the disease but were ecstatic to have a diagnosis and a treatment. Her hair had to be shaved, and she had daily medical baths and antibiotics and made a full recovery.

When Leo and Shasta joined us, Daisy immediately accepted them. She was never jealous or territorial. She was content with or without canine companionship. She was always compatible with any dogs that visited us or that she encountered in any circumstance.

Knowing When It's Time to Say Good-bye

Making the decision to terminate your animal companion's life is one of the most difficult decisions a pet lover will ever have to make. After all, your pet is a part of your family, and you don't euthanize human family members when they become ill or get old. A better way to approach this decision is to consider it akin to a "do not resuscitate" agreement. Under this agreement that you have with your pet, you would be entitled to make a decision on that animal's behalf as to when her suffering becomes too much or when her quality of life is so diminished that day-to-day existence would be miserable.

Of course you should communicate openly and honestly with your veterinarian, who can help you make this decision. Some of the factors that come into play when evaluating your pet's quality of life include the severity of her illness and the amount of medical attention she needs; whether or not she still eats regularly; the level of her physical comfort; and the amount of joy she gets out of being around those she is close to. Ultimately, no matter how difficult it is for you, her comfort and happiness should be your primary concern.

The years sped by. Daisy became diabetic soon after she became a senior, and I had to start giving her insulin daily. She was also on a restricted diet and ultimately lost her vision. I didn't change anything in the house or garage, and she was able to successfully navigate throughout both, even going through the doggy door. After a while, she stopped eating the prescription food, and her veterinarian and I agreed that I would cook certain foods for her. Eventually, I gave her anything she would eat, including ice cream. During this time I took her to the veterinarian frequently and found it very difficult to accept the reality that Daisy was near the end of her life. She seemed invincible to me, having survived three life-threatening situations: the man with the gun, a long excursion into the woods, and mange.

I knew I had to take action when she basically stopped eating and her back legs collapsed while she was drinking water. I

Daisy and me.

made an appointment to say good-bye to her on a Monday morning and spent the entire weekend with her. She did not appear to be in any discomfort, but her quality of life had decidedly diminished.

On our last night together, I stayed up just to watch her and be with her. I also held her for the final visit to the veterinarian. It was quick and peaceful. I took Daisy back home and laid her on the bed in a state of denial that it was time to say farewell. Finally the time came to wrap her in the satin comforter I had bought for my bed because her hair did not stick to it as much as to other fabrics. My sister Ruth and our friends Kathy and Teela had taken the day off from work to go with me to bury Daisy in the family cemetery in Sparta. I held Daisy wrapped in the comforter for the entire trip. At the cemetery I placed her in the casket, and we buried her beside her canine pal Leo.

I did not know how to live without Daisy and should have said good-bye a few days before I did. Besides my brother's death, being without Daisy was the saddest time I had ever experienced.

I understand why people who have this kind of emotional pain decide against adopting another dog, but I disagree with the decision. Because you learned the value of canine companionship from your departed friend, I think the greatest tribute you can pay to a beloved animal is to acknowledge her importance in your life by adopting other dogs in her memory. Another dog will not take the place of your lost companion but will make his or her own place in your heart. And don't ever forget that there are so many wonderful dogs waiting in shelters for a forever home.

I adopted Daisy to save her life. In going through the darkest days of my life, particularly after my brother Ray died, she saved mine. Daisy had a profound impact on my life. When I reflect on her adaptable and peaceful nature, I know that she was an inspiration to help me adapt to changes in my life—some I initiated and some I would not have chosen. She also helped me maintain a peaceful attitude toward people regardless of their actions. In situations that are potentially stressful, thinking about how Daisy approached life causes me to ask the question, "Will this really matter a year, or a month, or even a day from now?" Asking myself that question helps me to be more adaptable and accepting and at peace. I carry two photos in my wallet—one of my brother Ray and one of Daisy. She left her legacy with me and continues to impact my life positively.

LIFE LESSON:

Be adaptable and peaceful.

SINCE I FINISHED WRITING about the dogs in May 2008, we have seen a lot of changes. We said good-bye to Zeeke on January 22, 2009, and to Rocky on July 6, 2009. At www.LivingwiththeRescues.com I will tell you about our final "Zeeke Day" and how Rocky crossed over in Rocky style. I will also update you on the other dogs and how Daisy's Legacy is helping animals.

ACKNOWLEDGMENTS

MANY, MANY THANKS to my friends: Glynda Swift Farley, who kept the project confidential at my request, patiently read my handwriting, and sent the digital file to Suzanne and Mike Dickerson; and to Suzanne and Mike, who read the manuscript and made suggestions. Suzanne and Mike, owners of Remember This Photography, took photographs for the cover and some of the recent photographs. Suzanne created all the photo files that were sent to my publisher, Greenleaf Book Group LLC.

I am honored that Greenleaf Book Group accepted *Living With the Rescues: Life Lessons and Inspirations*. This is my first book and they were incredibly patient and supportive in guiding me through the process.

I appreciate and respect their Tree Neutral policy. I am most grateful for their commitment and enthusiasm for helping animals using the proceeds of this book.